Cambridge First Certificate in English 7

Examination papers from University of Cambridge ESOL Examinations: English for Speakers of Other Languages

CAMBRIDGE
UNIVERSITY PRESS

CAMBRIDGE UNIVERSITY PRESS
Cambridge, New York, Melbourne, Madrid, Cape Town, Singapore, São Paulo

Cambridge University Press
The Edinburgh Building, Cambridge CB2 2RU, UK

www.cambridge.org
Information on this title: www.cambridge.org/9780521611589

First published 2005

Printed in the United Kingdom at the University Press, Cambridge

A catalogue record for this book is available from the British Library

ISBN-13   978-0521-61158-9 Student's Book
ISBN-10   0-521-61158-X Student's Book

ISBN-13   978-0521-61159-6 Student's Book (with answers)
ISBN-10   0-521-61159-8 Student's Book (with answers)

ISBN-13   978-0521-61163-3 Set of 2 Cassettes
ISBN-10   0-521-61163-6 Set of 2 Cassettes

ISBN-13   978-0521-61162-6 Set of 2 Audio CDs
ISBN-10   0-521-61162-8 Set of 2 Audio CDs

ISBN-13   978-0521-61161-9 Self-study Pack
ISBN-10   0-521-61161-X Self-study Pack

Contents

Thanks and acknowledgements

The publishers are grateful to the following for permission to use copyright material. It has not been possible to identify the sources of all the material used and in such cases the publishers would welcome information from the copyright owners.

For the extract on p. 27 from 'Treasure Island' by Brian Pendreigh, published in *The Sunday Times* on 2nd August 1998 (C) NI Syndication; for the extract on p. 28 from *American Pastoral* by Philip Roth, published by Jonathan Cape. Copyright (C) 1997 by Philip Roth. Reprinted by permission of Houghton Mifflin Company. All rights reserved. And by permission of The Random House Group Limited in the British Commonwealth; for the extract on p. 51 from 'Risk' by John Vidal, published in *The Guardian* on 9 June 1999, and for the extract on p. 57 from 'Young Shoppers' by Frances Rickford, published in *The Guardian* on 21 September 1993, and for the text on p. 78 'The Runningman', with kind permission of Alex Bellos, published in *The Guardian* on 15 October 1999 (C) Guardian; for the article on p. 42 'Bigfoot', published in the *Daily Telegraph* Young Telegraph Supplement 13 Feb 1999, and for the text on p. 75 'Memory Test' by Jerome Burne, published in the *Sunday Telegraph* 26 Oct 1997 (C) Telegraph Group Limited; for the article on p. 76 'Acting minus the drama' by Benedicte Page, published in *The Bookseller* on 23 April 1999.

Colour section

ACESTOCK.COM for pp.C14/15, C14/15; Action Images for p.C6/C7; Alamy/James Frank for p.C5 (top), Alamy/Jim Pickerell for p.C10/C11; Anthony Blake Photo Library/ Eaglemoss for p.C14/15; Corbis for p.C13 (top), Corbis/Dave Bartruff for p.C6/C7, Corbis/Richard Olivier for p.C1. (bottom), Corbis/Phil Schermeister for p.C6/C7; Getty Images/Image Bank for pp.C6/C7, C14/15, Getty Images/Lonely Planet for p.C16 (top), Getty Images /Photodisc for pp.C6/C7, C13 (bottom), Getty Images/Stone for pp.C10/C11, C16 (bottom), Getty Images/Taxi for pp.C1 (top), C6/C7; Image State for p.C5 (bottom), Image State /AGE /Fotostock for p.C4 (bottom), Image State/Premium for p.C14/15; Life File/Emma Lee for p.C14/15, Life File/Jan Suttle for p.C1O/C11; Pictures Colour Library/Clive Sawyer for p.C12 (top), Pictures Colour Library/ PhotoLocation Ltd for p.C14/15, Pictures Colour Library/Picture Finders for p.C4 (top); PowerStock/Doug Scott for pp.C10/C11, C10/C11, PowerStock/HimsI for p.C6/C7, PowerStock/Javier Larrea for p.C10/C11, PowerStock /Richard G for p.C10/C11; PowerStockJ D Dallett for p.C8 (top); Rex Features/John Harmah for p.C8 (bottom), Rex Feature/SIPA Press for pp.C12 (bottom), C9 (top), C9 (bottom).

Artwork: Oxford Designers & Illustrators

Picture research by Valerie Mulcahy

Design concept by Peter Ducker

Cover design by Dunne & Scully

The recordings which accompany this book were made at Studio AVP, London.

Introduction

This collection of four complete practice tests comprises past papers from the University of Cambridge ESOL Examinations First Certificate in English (FCE) examination; students can practise these tests on their own or with the help of a teacher.

The FCE examination is part of a group of examinations developed by Cambridge ESOL called the Cambridge Main Suite. The Main Suite consists of five examinations that have similar characteristics but are designed for different levels of English language ability. Within the five levels, FCE is at Level B2 in the *Council of Europe's Common European Framework of Reference for Languages: Learning, teaching, assessment.* It has also been accredited by the Qualifications and Curriculum Authority in the UK as a Level 1 ESOL certificate in the National Qualifications Framework. The FCE examination is widely recognised in commerce and industry and in individual university faculties and other educational institutions.

Examination	Council of Europe Framework Level	UK National Qualifications Framework Level
CPE Certificate of Proficiency in English	C2	3
CAE Certificate in Advanced English	C1	2
FCE First Certificate in English	B2	1
PET Preliminary English Test	B1	Entry 3
KET Key English Test	A2	Entry 2

Further information

The information contained in this practice book is designed to be an overview of the exam. For a full description of all of the above exams including information about task types, testing focus and preparation, please see the relevant handbooks which can be obtained from Cambridge ESOL at the address below or from the website at: www.CambridgeESOL.org

University of Cambridge ESOL Examinations
1 Hills Road
Cambridge CB1 2EU
United Kingdom

Telephone: +44 1223 553355
Fax: +44 1223 460278
e-mail: ESOLHelpdesk@ucles.org.uk

The structure of FCE: an overview

The FCE examination consists of five papers.

Paper 1   Reading   1 hour 15 minutes
This paper consists of **four parts**. Each part contains a text and some questions. Part 4 may contain two or more shorter related texts. There are **35 questions** in total, including multiple choice, gapped text and matching questions.

Paper 2   Writing   1 hour 30 minutes
This paper consists of **two parts** which carry equal marks. For both parts candidates have to write between 120 and 180 words. Part 1 is **compulsory**. It provides texts which are sometimes accompanied by visual material to help in writing a letter.

In Part 2, there are four tasks from which candidates **choose one** to write about. The range of tasks from which questions may be drawn includes an article, a report, a composition, a short story and a letter. The last question is based on the set books. These books remain on the list for two or three years. Look on the website, or contact the Cambridge ESOL Local Secretary in your area for the up-to-date list of set books. The question on the set books has two options from which candidates **choose one** to write about.

Paper 3   Use of English   1 hour 15 minutes
This paper consists of **five parts** and tests control of English grammar, vocabulary and spelling. There are **65 questions** in total. The tasks include gap-filling exercises, sentence transformation, word formation and error correction.

Paper 4   Listening   40 minutes (approximately)
This paper contains **four parts**. Each part contains a recorded text or texts and some questions including multiple choice, sentence completion, true/false and matching. Each text is heard twice. There is a total of **30 questions**.

Paper 5   Speaking   14 minutes
This paper consists of **four parts**. The standard test format is two candidates and two examiners. One examiner takes part in the conversation, the other examiner listens and gives marks. Candidates will be given photographs and other visual material to look at and talk about. Sometimes candidates will talk with the other candidate, sometimes with the examiner and sometimes with both.

Grading

The overall FCE grade is based on the total score gained in all five papers. It is not necessary to achieve a satisfactory level in all five papers in order to pass the examination. Certificates are given to candidates who pass the examination with grade A, B or C. A is the highest. The minimum successful performance in order to achieve a grade C corresponds to about 60% of the total marks. D and E are failing grades. All candidates are sent a Statement of Results which includes a graphical profile of their performance in each paper and shows their relative performance in each one. Each paper is weighted to 40 marks. Therefore, the five FCE papers total 200 marks, after weighting.

For further information on grading and results, go to the website (see page v).

Test 1

PAPER 1   READING (1 hour 15 minutes)

Part 1

You are going to read a magazine article in which a famous chef talks about the importance of good service in restaurants. Choose the most suitable heading from the list **A–I** for each part (**1–7**) of the article. There is one extra heading you do not need to use. There is an example at the beginning (**0**).

Mark your answers **on the separate answer sheet**.

A	A central figure
B	A policy for the times
C	Seen but not heard
D	A fairer system
E	Playing the right part
F	Time well spent
G	A strong sense of involvement
H	The deciding factor
I	All-round improvement

At your service

Top chef and restaurant owner Giancarlo Curtis talks about what he looks for, apart from good food, when he eats out.

0	I

Recently, I went into a restaurant near my home where I have eaten several times over the years. It used to have old-fashioned traditional style, but it has just re-opened after being completely renovated. The new surroundings seem to have given a lift to everything, from the food cooked by a new chef from Brittany in France, to the atmosphere and the quality of the service.

1	

Many hours of behind-the-scenes work must have gone into getting the service so good. The staff were very pleasant and the speed with which they reacted to customers' needs was excellent. When someone sneezed, a box of tissues appeared. I have never seen that before in a restaurant. The preparation has certainly paid off.

2	

Twenty years ago when people went out to restaurants, they probably never set eyes on the chef – probably didn't even know his name. But the person they did know was the head waiter. He was the important one, the person who could get you the best table, who could impress your friends by recognising you when you arrived.

3	

Things have changed, but I think what is going to happen with so many good new restaurants opening these days is that the waiters are going to become very important again. The level of service is what is going to distinguish one restaurant from another.

4	

But we are talking about modern, unstuffy service, which is not four waiters hovering around your table making you nervous, but a relaxed presence, giving you the feeling there is someone there and providing help and advice when you need it. There is a fine distinction between a server and a servant, and this is what the best waiter has learnt to appreciate.

5	

Although they have to be commercial, the most popular restaurants aim to provide the kind of reception, comfort and consideration you would give to someone coming for a dinner party at your home. Service is not about the correctness of knives and forks and glasses – people really don't care about those things any more – nowadays it is about putting people at their ease.

6	

What's more, waiting staff need to have a stake in the success of the enterprise. I realised that when I opened my own restaurant. The staff, chefs and waiters did all the decorating and the flowers themselves and it worked well because the right atmosphere had been created by people who cared.

7	

Above all, the waiting staff should be consistent, which is why I have always preferred the custom of putting an optional service charge on the bill, rather than relying on discretionary tips, so that all the staff feel valued. I don't like the kind of situation where there is competition going on, with one star waiter trying to outshine the rest. That affects the quality of the service as a whole.

Part 2

You are going to read a magazine article about an artist who paints flowers. For questions **8–14**, choose the answer (**A**, **B**, **C** or **D**) which you think fits best according to the text.

Mark your answers **on the separate answer sheet**.

An eye for detail

Artist Susan Shepherd is best known for her flower paintings, and the large garden that surrounds her house is the source of many of her subjects. It is full of her favourite flowers, most especially varieties of tulips and poppies. Some of the plants are unruly and seed themselves all over the garden. There is a harmony of colour, shape and structure in the two long flower borders that line the paved path which crosses the garden from east to west. *line 12* Much of this is due to the previous owners, who were keen gardeners, and who left plants that appealed to Susan. She also inherited the gardener, Danny. 'In fact, it was really his garden,' she says. 'We got on very well. At first he would say, "Oh, it's not worth it" to some of the things I wanted to put in, but when I said I wanted to paint them, he recognised what I had in mind.'

Susan prefers to focus on detailed studies of individual plants rather than on the garden as a whole, though she will occasionally paint a group of plants where they are. More usually, she picks them and then takes them up to her studio. 'I don't set the whole thing up at once,' she says. 'I take one flower out and paint it, which might take a few days, and then I bring in another one and build up the painting that way. Sometimes it takes a couple of years to finish.'

Her busiest time of year is spring and early summer, when the tulips are out, followed by the poppies. 'They all come out together, and you're so busy,' she says. But the gradual decaying process is also part of the fascination for her. With tulips, for example, 'you bring them in and put them in water, then leave them for perhaps a day and they each form themselves into different shapes. They open out and are fantastic. When you first put them in a vase, you think they are boring, but they change all the time with twists and turns.'

Susan has always been interested in plants: 'I did botany at school and used to collect wild flowers from all around the countryside,' she says. 'I wasn't particularly interested in gardening then; in fact, I didn't like garden flowers, I thought they were artificial – to me, the only real ones were wild.' Nowadays, the garden owes much to plants that originated in far-off lands, though they seem as much at home in her garden as they did in China or the Himalayas. She has a come-what-may attitude to the garden, rather like an affectionate aunt who is quite happy for children to run about undisciplined as long as they don't do any serious damage.

With two forthcoming exhibitions to prepare for, and a ready supply of subject material at her back door, finding time to work in the garden has been difficult recently. She now employs an extra gardener but, despite the need to paint, she knows that, to maintain her connection with her subject matter, 'you have to get your hands dirty'.

8 In the first paragraph, the writer describes Susan's garden as

    A having caused problems for the previous owners.
    B having a path lined with flowers.
    C needing a lot of work to keep it looking attractive.
    D being only partly finished.

9 What does 'this' in line 12 refer to?

    A the position of the path
    B the number of wild plants
    C the position of the garden
    D the harmony of the planting

10 What does Susan say about Danny?

    A He felt she was interfering in his work.
    B He immediately understood her feelings.
    C He was recommended by the previous owners.
    D He was slow to see the point of some of her ideas.

11 What is Susan's approach to painting?

    A She will wait until a flower is ready to be picked before painting it.
    B She likes to do research on a plant before she paints it.
    C She spends all day painting an individual flower.
    D She creates her paintings in several stages.

12 Susan thinks that tulips

    A are more colourful and better shaped than other flowers.
    B are not easy to paint because they change so quickly.
    C look best some time after they have been cut.
    D should be kept in the house for as long as possible.

13 How does the writer describe Susan's attitude to her garden?

    A She thinks children should be allowed to enjoy it.
    B She prefers planting wild flowers from overseas.
    C She likes a certain amount of disorder.
    D She dislikes criticism of her planting methods.

14 What point is Susan making in the final paragraph?

    A It's essential to find the time to paint even if there is gardening to be done.
    B It's important not to leave the gardening entirely to other people.
    C It's good to have expert help when you grow plants.
    D It's hard to do exhibitions if there are not enough plants ready in the garden.

Part 3

You are going to read a magazine article about swimming with dolphins. Eight paragraphs have been removed from the article. Choose from the paragraphs **A–I** the one which fits each gap (**15–21**). There is one extra paragraph which you do not need to use. There is an example at the beginning (**0**).

Mark your answers **on the separate answer sheet**.

Dolphins in the Bay of Plenty

Swimming with groups of dolphins, known as 'pods', is becoming a popular holiday activity for the adventurous tourist. Our travel correspondent reports.

'You must remember that these dolphins are wild. They are not fed or trained in any way. These trips are purely on the dolphins' terms.' So said one of our guides, as she briefed us before we set out for our rendezvous.

0	I

No skill is required to swim with dolphins, just common sense and an awareness that we are visitors in their world. Once on board the boat, our guides talked to us about what we could expect from our trip.

15	

The common dolphin we were seeking has a blue-black upper body, a grey lower body, and a long snout. We had been told that if they were in a feeding mood we would get a short encounter with them, but if they were being playful then it could last as long as two hours.

16	

Soon we were in the middle of a much larger pod, with dolphins all around us. The first group of six swimmers put on their snorkels, slipped off the back of the boat and swam off towards them.

17	

Visibility was not at its best, but the low clicking sounds and the high-pitched squeaks were amazing enough. The dolphins did not seem bothered by my presence in the water above them. Sometimes they would rush by so close that I could feel the pressure-wave as they passed.

18	

I personally found it more rewarding to sit on the bow of the boat and watch as the surface of the sea all around filled with their perfectly arching dolphin backs. Some of the more advanced snorkellers were able to dive down with these dolphins, an experience they clearly enjoyed.

19	

In fact, they are very sociable animals, always supporting each other within the pod. The guides are beginning to recognise some of the local dolphins by the markings on their backs, and some individuals appear time after time.

20	

Indeed, the pod we had found, on some hidden signal, suddenly turned away from the boat and headed off in the same direction at high speed. We watched as hundreds of backs broke through the water's surface at the same time, disappearing into the distance.

21	

They had finally finished feeding and were content to play alongside as they showed us the way home. The sun beamed down, and as each dolphin broke the surface of the water and exhaled, a rainbow would form for a few seconds in the mist. It was an enchanting experience.

A   This was a magical experience and, as time in the water is limited, everyone rotates to get an equal share. We spent the next two hours getting in and out of the boat, and visiting other pods.

B   An excited shriek led us all to try something that one girl had just discovered, and we all rushed to hang our feet over the front so that the playful creatures would touch them.

C   A spotter plane circled above the bay, looking for large pods of dolphins to direct us towards. On deck, we watched for splashes on the surface of the water.

D   These include mothers gently guiding their young alongside, either to introduce them to the boat, or to proudly show off their babies. Yet, when they become bored with playing, they leave.

E   After 20 minutes, we sighted our first small pod. The dolphins came rushing towards the boat, swimming alongside and overtaking us until they could surf on the boat's bow wave.

F   However, touching the creatures is strongly discouraged. This is despite the fact that dolphins have a very friendly reputation, and have never been known to be aggressive towards human beings in the wild.

G   Eventually it was time to leave, and the boat headed back to port. As we slowly motored along, we picked up another pod, which was joined by more and more dolphins until we had a huge escort.

H   After five minutes, that group was signalled back to the boat. I got ready to slide into the water with the next six swimmers, leaving the excited chatter of the first group behind.

I   I was in Whakatane, in the Bay of Plenty in New Zealand, which is fast becoming the place to visit for those who want a close encounter with dolphins.

Part 4

You are going to read a magazine article in which five people talk about railway journeys. For questions **22–35**, choose from the people (**A–E**). The people may be chosen more than once. When more than one answer is required, these may be given in any order. There is an example at the beginning (**0**).

Mark your answers **on the separate answer sheet**.

Which person or people

found on returning years later that nothing had changed?	**0**	E
was unable to count on the train service?	**22**	
enjoyed the company of fellow passengers?	**23**	
found the views from the train dramatic?	**24**	**25**
welcomed a chance to relax on the trip?	**26**	
was never disappointed by the journey?	**27**	
has a reason for feeling grateful to one special train?	**28**	
travelled on a railway which is no longer in regular service?	**29**	
regretted not going on a particular train trip?	**30**	
used to travel on the railway whenever possible?	**31**	
learnt an interesting piece of information on a train journey?	**32**	
took a train which travelled from one country to another?	**33**	
says that the railway had been looked after by unpaid helpers?	**34**	
was once considered not old enough to travel by train?	**35**	

On the rails

Five celebrities tell Andrew Morgan their favourite memories of railway journeys.

A Andrea Thompson – Newsreader

I fell in love with the south of France a long time ago and try to get back there as often as I can. There's a local train from Cannes along the coast which crosses the border with Italy. It takes you past some of the most amazing seascapes. It never matters what the weather is like, or what time of the year it is, it is always enchanting. Out of the other window are some of the best back gardens and residences in the whole of France. You feel like someone peeping into the property of the rich and famous. The travellers themselves are always lively because there is an interesting mix of tourists and locals, all with different itineraries but all admirers of the breathtaking journey.

B Rod Simpson – Explorer

I have enjoyed so many rail journeys through the years, but if I had to pick a favourite it would be the Nile Valley Express, which runs across the desert of northern Sudan. The one misfortune in my youth, growing up in South Africa, was missing out on a family train journey from Cape Town to the Kruger National Park. I was regarded as being too young and troublesome and was sent off to an aunt. When I came to live in England as a teenager, I still hadn't travelled by train. London Waterloo was the first real station I ever saw and its great glass dome filled me with wonder.

C Betty Cooper – Novelist

I am indebted to one train in particular: the Blue Train, which took my husband and me on our honeymoon across France to catch a boat to Egypt. It was on the train that my husband gave me a pink dress, which I thought was absolutely wonderful. Someone happened to mention that pink was good for the brain, and I've never stopped wearing the colour since. What I remember about the journey itself, however, is how lovely it was to travel through France and then by boat up the Nile to Luxor. It was, without a doubt, the perfect way to wind down after all the wedding preparations.

D Martin Brown – Journalist

We were working on a series of articles based on a round-the-world trip and had to cross a desert in an African country. There wasn't a road, so the only way we could continue our journey was to take what was affectionately known as the Desert Express. The timetable was unreliable – we were just given a day. We also heard that, in any case, the driver would often wait for days to depart if he knew there were passengers still on their way. When it appeared, there was a sudden charge of what seemed like hundreds of people climbing into and onto the carriages – passengers were even allowed to travel on the roof free. During the night, the train crossed some of the most beautiful landscapes I have ever seen. It was like a dream, like travelling across the moon.

E Jennifer Dickens – Actress

I imagine most people's favourite impressions of trains and railways are formed when they are young children, but that's not my case. I was brought up in Singapore and Cyprus, where I saw very few trains, let alone travelled on them. It wasn't until I was a teenager that trains began to dominate my life. I made a film which featured a railway in Yorkshire. Most of the filming took place on an old, disused stretch of the line which had been lovingly maintained by volunteers. That's where my passion for steam trains began. When we weren't filming, we took every opportunity to have a ride on the train, and, when I went back last year, it was as if time had stood still. Everything was the same, even the gas lights on the station platform!

PAPER 2   WRITING (1 hour 30 minutes)

Part 1

You **must** answer this question.

1   Your English friend, Bill, is a travel writer and he recently visited a town which you know well. He has written a chapter about the town for a guide book and you have just read the chapter.

Read the extract from Bill's letter and your notes. Then, using all your notes, write a letter to Bill, giving him the information and suggestions he needs.

> *Thanks for agreeing to check the chapter that I've written. Could you let me know what you liked about it? If any of the information is inaccurate, please give me the correct information! Do you think there's anything else I should include?*
>
> *Once again, thanks a lot for reading the chapter. Please write back soon.*
>
> *Bill*

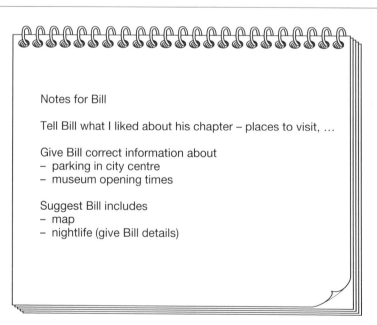

Notes for Bill

Tell Bill what I liked about his chapter – places to visit, …

Give Bill correct information about
– parking in city centre
– museum opening times

Suggest Bill includes
– map
– nightlife (give Bill details)

Write a **letter** of between **120** and **180** words in an appropriate style.
Do not write any postal addresses.

Part 2

Write an answer to **one** of the questions **2–5** in this part. Write your answer in **120–180** words in an appropriate style.

___

2   Your teacher has asked you to write a story for the college English language magazine. The story must **begin** with the following words:

It was only a small mistake but it changed my life for ever.   *H.W -*

Write your **story**.

3   You see the following notice in an international magazine.

COMPETITION

Is it better to live in a flat, a modern house or an old house?

Write us an article giving your opinions.

The best article will be published and the writer will receive £500.

Write your **article** for the magazine.

4   You have had a class discussion on being rich and famous. Your teacher has now asked you to write a composition, giving your opinions on the following statement:

Everybody would like to be rich and famous.

Write your **composition**.

5   Answer **one** of the following two questions based on your reading of **one** of these set books. Write **(a)** or **(b)** as well as the number **5** in the question box, and the **title** of the book next to the box. Your answer **must** be about one of the books below.

Best Detective Stories of Agatha Christie – Longman Fiction
A Tale of Two Cities – Charles Dickens
Animal Farm – George Orwell
More Tales from Shakespeare – Charles and Mary Lamb
Round the World in Eighty Days – Jules Verne

Either **(a)** Which event in the book made the strongest impression on you? Write a **composition** for your teacher describing this event and explaining why it had such an effect on you, with reference to the book or one of the short stories you have read.

Or **(b)** 'I learnt a lot about how people think and behave from one of the characters in the book.' Do you agree with this statement? Write a **composition**, referring to one of the characters in the book or one of the short stories you have read.

PAPER 3   USE OF ENGLISH (1 hour 15 minutes)

Part 1

For questions **1–15**, read the text below and decide which answer (**A**, **B**, **C** or **D**) best fits each space. There is an example at the beginning (**0**).

Mark your answers **on the separate answer sheet.**

Example:

0   A joined   **B** held   **C** were   **D** took

0	A	B	C	D
	⌐	⌐	⌐	▬

THOMAS EDISON

On the night of 21 October 1931, millions of Americans **(0)** ….. part in a coast-to-coast ceremony to commemorate the passing of a great man. Lights **(1)** ….. in homes and offices from New York to California. The ceremony **(2)** ….. the death of an inventor – indeed, to many people, the most important inventor of **(3)** ….. time: Thomas Alva Edison.

Few inventors have **(4)** ….. an impact as great as his on everyday life. While most of his 1,000-plus inventions were devices we no **(5)** ….. use, many of the things he invented played a crucial **(6)** ….. in the development of modern technology, simply by showing what was possible. And one should never **(7)** ….. how amazing some of Edison's inventions were.

In so many ways, Edison is the perfect example of an inventor, by which I **(8)** ….. not just someone who **(9)** ….. up clever gadgets, but someone whose products transform the lives of millions. He possessed the key characteristics that an inventor needs to **(10)** ….. a success of inventions. Sheer determination is certainly one of them. Edison famously tried thousands of materials while working **(11)** ….. a new type of battery, reacting to failure by cheerfully **(12)** ….. to his colleagues: 'Well, **(13)** ….. we know 8,000 things that don't work.' Knowing when to take no **(14)** ….. of experts is also important. Edison's proposal for electric lighting circuitry was **(15)** ….. with total disbelief by eminent scientists, until he lit up whole streets with his lights.

1 **A** turned out   **B** came off   **C** went out   **D** put off

2 **A** marked   **B** distinguished   **C** noted   **D** indicated

3 **A** whole   **B** full   **C** entire   **D** all

4 **A** put   **B** had   **C** served   **D** set

5 **A** further   **B** later   **C** wider   **D** longer

6 **A** effect   **B** place   **C** role   **D** share

7 **A** underestimate   **B** lower   **C** decrease   **D** mislead

8 **A** mean   **B** think   **C** suppose   **D** express

9 **A** creates   **B** shapes   **C** dreams   **D** forms

10 **A** gain   **B** make   **C** achieve   **D** get

11 **A** up   **B** through   **C** on   **D** to

12 **A** announcing   **B** informing   **C** instructing   **D** notifying

13 **A** by far   **B** at least   **C** even though   **D** for all

14 **A** notice   **B** regard   **C** attention   **D** view

15 **A** gathered   **B** caught   **C** drawn   **D** received

Part 2

For questions **16–30**, read the text below and think of the word which best fits each space. Use only **one** word in each space. There is an example at the beginning (**0**).

Write your answers **on the separate answer sheet**.

Example: | **0** | *after*

VANCOUVER

Vancouver in western Canada is named **(0)** ..*after*.. Captain George Vancouver of the British Royal Navy. However, Captain Vancouver was not the first European **(16)** ……….. visit the area. The coast **(17)** ……….. already been explored by the Spanish. Captain Vancouver did **(18)** ……….. spend many days there, even **(19)** ……….. he was warmly welcomed by the local people and the scenery amazed him and everyone else **(20)** ……….. was travelling with him.

The scenery still amazes visitors to **(21)** ……….. city of Vancouver today. First-time visitors who are **(22)** ……….. search of breathtaking views **(23)** ……….. usually directed to a beach which is about ten minutes **(24)** ……….. the city centre. There, looking out over the sailing boats racing across the blue water, visitors see Vancouver's towering skyline backed by the magnificent Coast Mountains. Then they sigh and say, 'It's **(25)** ……….. beautiful that I want to stay forever!'

You can't blame them. The city is regularly picked by international travel associations **(26)** ……….. one of the world's best tourist destinations. They are only confirming what the two million residents and eight million tourists visiting Greater Vancouver **(27)** ……….. single year already know: there is simply **(28)** ……….. other place on earth quite **(29)** ……….. it. It's not just the gorgeous setting where mountains meet the sea that appeals to people, **(30)** ……….. also Vancouver's wide range of sporting, cultural and entertainment facilities.

Part 3

For questions **31–40**, complete the second sentence so that it has a similar meaning to the first sentence, using the word given. **Do not change the word given**. You must use between **two** and **five** words, including the word given.

Here is an example (**0**).

Example:

0   A very friendly taxi driver drove us into town.

   driven

   We .... a very friendly taxi driver.

The space can be filled by the words 'were driven into town by' so you write:

0	*were driven into town by*

Write **only** the missing words **on the separate answer sheet**.

---

31   'Don't sit in front of the computer for too long,' our teacher told us.

   warned

   Our teacher .... in front of the computer for too long.

32   We got lost coming home from the leisure centre.

   way

   We couldn't .... from the leisure centre.

33   I tried as hard as I could to keep my promise to them.

   best

   I .... break my promise to them.

34   Mary didn't find it difficult to pass her driving test.

   difficulty

   Mary had .... her driving test.

35 I always trust Carla's advice.

somebody

Carla .... advice I always trust.

36 We appear to have been given the wrong address.

as

It .... we have been given the wrong address.

37 I couldn't understand the instructions for my new video recorder.

sense

The instructions for my new video recorder didn't ....
me.

38 Stephen didn't realise that the city centre was a bus ride away.

necessary

What Stephen failed to realise .... to catch a bus to the
city centre.

39 It's a pity we didn't do more sport when I was at school.

could

I wish that .... more sport when I was at school.

40 He described the hotel to us in detail.

detailed

He .... of the hotel.

Part 4

For questions **41–55**, read the text below and look carefully at each line. Some of the lines are correct, and some have a word which should not be there.

If a line is correct, put a tick (✓) by the number **on the separate answer sheet**. If a line has a word which should **not** be there, write the word **on the separate answer sheet**. There are two examples at the beginning (**0** and **00**).

0	✓

Examples:

00	*like*

FRIENDSHIP

0	I believe that nothing matters as much as having a couple of really good
00	friends. They help you feel like good about yourself and they'll always
41	listen to your problems for hours on end. Since there are friends for different
42	reasons, for different ages and stages in life. New made friends and 'best'
43	friends, friends for playing tennis and going to the cinema with – all
44	of us are dependent on having friends. So how and why do we make up
45	friends? Psychologists tell us that we prefer those we see as sharing with
46	our views and attitudes and who are similar to us in an age and background,
47	though not necessarily in any personality. We see our friends as reflecting
48	ourselves, or that what we would like to be. This can be particularly
49	important when we are teenagers. Many of people – and I'm no exception –
50	regard their oldest friends as their closest. I have a friend so that
51	I've known since some schooldays. She lives in Australia and we
52	rarely see much each other. However, on my last birthday we got together
53	in Paris and have spent a wonderful weekend sightseeing and talking.
54	We will know that, no matter how many years go by when we do not
55	get together at all, the same level of friendship always remains.

Part 5

For questions **56–65**, read the text below. Use the word given in capitals at the end of each line to form a word that fits in the space in the **same** line. There is an example at the beginning (**0**).

Write your answers **on the separate answer sheet**.

Example:

0	*amazement*

A JOB WITH RISKS

Have you ever been to the cinema and wondered in (**0**) *amazement* how   **AMAZE**

film stars manage to perform (**56**) .... acts like jumping off buildings or driving   **DANGER**

at great speed? They don't, of course. The real (**57**) .... are usually stunt men   **PERFORM**

or women, who can earn a very good (**58**) .... by standing in   **LIVE**

for the stars when necessary. The work is (**59**) .... demanding and, before   **INCREDIBLE**

qualifying for this job, they have to (**60**) .... their ability in six sports including **PROOF**

skiing, riding and gymnastics.

Naturally, (**61**) .... and timing are important and everything is planned down   **SAFE**

to the (**62**) .... detail. In a scene which involves a complicated series of   **TINY**

actions, there is no time for (**63**) .... mistakes. A stunt man or woman often   **CARE**

has only one chance of getting things right, (**64**) .... film stars, who can   **LIKE**

always film a scene (**65**) .... until it gains the director's approval.   **REPEAT**

PAPER 4   LISTENING (approximately 40 minutes)

Part 1

You will hear people talking in eight different situations. For questions **1–8**, choose the best answer (**A**, **B** or **C**).

1   You overhear a young man talking about his first job.
    How did he feel in his first job?

   A   bored

   B   confused

   C   enthusiastic

| | 1 |

2   You hear a radio announcement about a dance company.
    What are listeners being invited to?

   A   a show

   B   a talk

   C   a party

| | 2 |

3   You overhear a woman talking to a man about something that happened to her.
    Who was she?

   A   a pedestrian

   B   a driver

   C   a passenger

| | 3 |

4   You hear a woman talking on the radio about her work making wildlife films.
    What is her main point?

   A   Being in the right place at the right time is a matter of luck.

   B   More time is spent planning than actually filming.

   C   It is worthwhile spending time preparing.

| | 4 |

5 You hear part of a travel programme on the radio.
Where is the speaker?

A outside a café

B by the sea

C on a lake

5

6 You overhear a woman talking about a table-tennis table in a sports shop.
What does she want the shop assistant to do about her table-tennis table?

A provide her with a new one

B have it put together for her

C give her the money back

6

7 You hear part of an interview with a businesswoman.
What is her business?

A hiring out boats

B hiring out caravans

C building boats

7

8 You hear a man talking on the radio.
Who is talking?

A an actor

B a journalist

C a theatre-goer

8

Part 2

You will hear a radio interview with Mike Reynolds, whose hobby is exploring underground places such as caves. For questions **9–18**, complete the sentences.

Cavers explore underground places such as mines and

| | 9 | as well as caves.

When cavers camp underground, they choose places which have

| | *and* | 10 | available.

In the UK, the place Mike likes best for caving is | | 11 |

As a physical activity, Mike compares caving to | | 12 |

Cavers can pay as much as £20 for a suitable | | 13 |

Cavers can pay as much as £50 for the right kind of

| | 14 |, which is worn on the head.

Mike recommends buying expensive

| | 15 | to avoid having accidents.

Caving is a sport for people of | | 16 | and backgrounds.

Some caves in Britain are called 'places of | | ' | 17 |

The need for safety explains why people don't organise caving

| | 18 |

Part 3

You will hear five different people talking about their work on a cruise ship. For questions **19–23**, choose from the list (**A–F**) what each speaker says about their work. Use the letters only once. There is one extra letter which you do not need to use.

A   One aspect of my job is less interesting than others.

<table>
<tr><td>Speaker 1</td><td></td><td>19</td></tr>
</table>

B   My job involves planning for the unexpected.

<table>
<tr><td>Speaker 2</td><td></td><td>20</td></tr>
</table>

C   You have to be sociable to do my job.

<table>
<tr><td>Speaker 3</td><td></td><td>21</td></tr>
</table>

D   I don't like routine in my working life.

<table>
<tr><td>Speaker 4</td><td></td><td>22</td></tr>
</table>

E   There's not much work to do during the day.

<table>
<tr><td>Speaker 5</td><td></td><td>23</td></tr>
</table>

F   I provide passengers with a souvenir of their trip.

Part 4

You will hear a radio discussion in which four people are talking about the advertising of children's toys on television. For questions **24–30**, decide which views are expressed by any of the speakers and which are not. Write **YES** for those views which are expressed, and **NO** for those which are not expressed.

24 Most young children are aware when advertisements are being shown on television. `[    ] 24`

25 There are fewer toy advertisements on British television than there used to be. `[    ] 25`

26 Parents are spending increasing amounts of their money on traditional toys. `[    ] 26`

27 Advertisers have to indicate the actual size of toys advertised on television. `[    ] 27`

28 Children would be less influenced by toy advertisements if they were only shown after 8.00 pm. `[    ] 28`

29 Advertising encourages children to lose interest in their toys very quickly. `[    ] 29`

30 Evidence shows that most people are worried about toy advertising on television. `[    ] 30`

PAPER 5   SPEAKING (14 minutes)

You take the Speaking test with another candidate, referred to here as your partner. There are two examiners. One will speak to you and your partner and the other will be listening. Both examiners will award marks.

Part 1 (3 minutes)

The examiner asks you and your partner questions about yourselves. You may be asked about things like 'your home town', 'your interests', 'your career plans', etc.

Part 2 (4 minutes)

The examiner gives you two photographs and asks you to talk about them for one minute. The examiner then asks your partner a question about your photographs and your partner responds briefly.

Then the examiner gives your partner two different photographs. Your partner talks about these photographs for one minute. This time the examiner asks you a question about your partner's photographs and you respond briefly.

Part 3 (approximately 3 minutes)

The examiner asks you and your partner to talk together. You may be asked to solve a problem or try to come to a decision about something. For example, you might be asked to decide the best way to use some rooms in a language school. The examiner gives you a picture to help you but does not join in the conversation.

Part 4 (approximately 4 minutes)

The examiner joins in the conversation. You all talk together in a more general way about what has been said in Part 3. The examiner asks you questions but you and your partner are also expected to develop the conversation.

Test 2

PAPER 1   READING (1 hour 15 minutes)

Part 1

You are going to read a newspaper article about an island in the Irish Sea, called the Isle of Man, which is fast becoming a centre for film-making. Choose from the list **A–H** the sentence which best summarises each part (**1–6**) of the article. There is one extra sentence which you do not need to use. There is an example at the beginning (**0**).

Mark your answers **on the separate answer sheet**.

A	The new film industry is not expected to make big profits immediately.
B	The new film industry has resulted in some criticism of the island's government.
C	It was initially difficult to persuade film-makers to use the island.
D	The island is already able to compete with other film-making centres.
E	Film-makers are able to find a wide range of settings for their films on the island.
F	More investment is planned as the new film industry becomes established.
G	Financial reasons have made film companies see the island as a good place to make new films.
H	The island's inhabitants are keen to be involved with the new film industry.

TREASURE ISLAND

0	H

Only 73,000 people live on the Isle of Man, but several thousand of them have registered with Jay-Dee Promotions. This is the casting and extras agency John Banks and his wife Pat run to service the film industry that has suddenly taken off on the island. Banks does not know exactly how many clients he has – he is too busy to count them. And Jay-Dee is only one of three such agencies that have sprung up in the last year or two.

1	

Until recently the island's principal contributions to cinema were a comedy about motorcycle racing, and *The Manxman*, one of Alfred Hitchcock's silent movies. But producers have now discovered an important reason to undertake the inconvenient voyage to the middle of the Irish Sea – money. In the past couple of years, the Isle of Man government has lent over £6.5 million of public money to film companies. If a film is a success then the Isle of Man will receive a share of the profits. This has turned the island into an offshore Hollywood.

2	

Only one film was made in 1995, two in 1996, but there were no fewer than eleven in the following year. However, from the beginning, the Isle of Man government has followed the strategy of Hollywood, where the rule of thumb is that for every ten films, seven will lose money, one will cover its costs, one will provide modest returns, and the tenth, it is hoped, will be an enormous hit.

3	

An island 45 kilometres long, with no history of film production, is suddenly turning out the same number of films as the Scottish film industry, which has a huge pool of local talent and an infrastructure that has evolved over the years. However, it was always the intention of the Isle of Man government to lure productions away from England, Scotland and Ireland.

4	

Producers have suddenly discovered the affluent little holiday island to be the perfect location for seemingly any film. It has doubled for Cornwall, Hamburg, Sydney Harbour in the nineteenth century, rural Ireland and inner-city England. It has even attracted a new production of *Treasure Island*. Geographical specifics did not seem to be uppermost in the mind of the film's producer: 'We gambled with the fact that we would be able to have enough sunny days to be able to do the tropical island part.'

5	

The Isle of Man film initiative was inspired not by vague dreams of glory, but by hopes of boosting the economy. Its tourist industry has been in decline for twenty years and it was thought that a hit film would help it. One of the early objectives was simply to demonstrate to a doubtful film industry that it was possible to make feature films on the island.

6	

The government's financial advisors have targeted films in the £2–3 million price range as promising the highest potential returns at least risk. The Isle of Man is an important financial centre and this expertise has aided its move into film. The island's government has another £6.5 million to lend over the next two years and is currently considering building a studio.

Part 2

You are going to read an extract from a novel. For questions **7–13**, choose the answer (**A**, **B**, **C** or **D**) which you think fits best according to the text.

Mark your answers **on the separate answer sheet**.

Miss Rita Cohen, a tiny, pale-skinned girl who looked half the age of Seymour's daughter, Marie, but claimed to be some six years older, came to his factory one day. She was dressed in overalls and ugly big shoes, and a bush of wiry hair framed her pretty face. She was so tiny, so young that he could barely believe that she was at the University of Pennsylvania, doing research into the leather industry in New Jersey for her Master's degree.

Three or four times a year someone either phoned Seymour or wrote to him to ask permission to see his factory, and occasionally he would assist a student by answering questions over the phone or, if the student struck him as especially serious, by offering a brief tour.

Rita Cohen was nearly as small, he thought, as the children from Marie's third-year class, who'd been brought the 50 kilometres from their rural schoolhouse one day, all those years ago, so that Marie's daddy could show them how he made gloves, show them especially Marie's favourite spot, the laying-off table, where, at the end of the process, the men shaped and pressed each and every glove by pulling it carefully down over steam-heated brass hands. The hands were dangerously hot and they were shiny and they stuck straight up from the table in a row, thin-looking, like hands that had been flattened. As a little girl, Marie was captivated by their strangeness and called them the 'pancake hands'.

He heard Rita asking, 'How many pieces come in a shipment?' 'How many? Between twenty and twenty-five thousand.' She continued taking notes as she asked, 'They come direct to your shipping department?'

He liked finding that she was interested in every last detail. 'They come to the tannery. The tannery is a contractor. We buy the material and they make it into the right kind of leather for us to use. My grandfather and father worked in the tannery right here in town. So did I, for six months, when I started in the business. Ever been inside a tannery?' 'Not yet.' 'Well, you've got to go to a tannery if you're going to write about leather. I'll set that up for you if you'd like that. They're primitive places. The technology has improved things, but what you'll see isn't that different from what you'd have seen hundreds of years ago. Awful work. It's said to be the oldest industry of which remains have been found anywhere. Six-thousand-year-old relics of tanning found somewhere – Turkey, I believe. The first clothing was just skins that were tanned by smoking them. I told you it was an interesting subject once you get into it. My father is the leather scholar; he's the one you should be talking to. Start my father off about gloves and he'll talk for two days. That's typical, by the way: glovemen love the trade and everything about it. Tell me, have you ever seen anything being manufactured, Miss Cohen?' 'I can't say I have.' 'Never seen anything made?' 'Saw my mother make a cake when I was a child.'

He laughed. She had made him laugh. An innocent with spirit, eager to learn. His daughter was easily 30 cm taller than Rita Cohen, fair where she was dark, but otherwise Rita Cohen had begun to remind him of Marie. The good-natured intelligence that would just waft out of her and into the house when she came home from school, full of what she'd learned in class. How she remembered everything. Everything neatly taken down in her notebook and memorised overnight.

'I'll tell you what we're going to do. We're going to bring you right through the whole process. Come on. We're going to make you a pair of gloves and you're going to watch them being made from start to finish. What size do you wear?'

7   What was Seymour's first impression of Rita Cohen?

    A   She reminded him of his daughter.
    B   She was rather unattractive.
    C   She did not look like a research student.
    D   She hadn't given much thought to her appearance.

8   Seymour would show students round his factory if

    A   he thought they were genuinely interested.
    B   they telephoned for permission.
    C   they wrote him an interesting letter.
    D   their questions were hard to answer by phone.

9   What did Seymour's daughter like most about visiting the factory?

    A   watching her father make gloves
    B   helping to shape the gloves
    C   making gloves for her schoolfriends
    D   seeing the brass hands

10   The word 'shiny' in line 14 describes

    A   the look of the hands.
    B   the size of the hands.
    C   the feel of the hands.
    D   the temperature of the hands.

11   Seymour says that most tanneries today

    A   have been running for over a hundred years.
    B   are located in very old buildings.
    C   are dependent on older workers.
    D   still use traditional methods.

12   What does Seymour admire about his father?

    A   his educational background
    B   his knowledge of history
    C   his enthusiasm for the business
    D   his skill as a glovemaker

13   When she was a schoolgirl, Marie

    A   made her parents laugh.
    B   was intelligent but lazy.
    C   easily forgot what she had learned.
    D   was hard-working and enthusiastic.

Part 3

You are going to read a newspaper article about human beings getting taller. Eight sentences have been removed from the article. Choose from the sentences **A–I** the one that fits each gap (**14–20**). There is one extra sentence which you do not need to use. There is an example at the beginning (**0**).

Mark your answers **on the separate answer sheet**.

It's true – we're all getting too big for our boots

Chris Greener was fourteen when he told his careers teacher he wanted to join the navy when he left school. 'What do you want to be?' asked the teacher, looking the boy up and down. 'The flagpole on a ship?' The teacher had a point – because Chris, though still only fourteen, was already almost two metres tall. **0** | **I**

Every decade, the average height of people in Europe grows another centimetre. Every year, more and more truly big people are born. Intriguingly, this does not mean humanity is producing a new super race. **14** Only now are we losing the effects of generations of poor diet – with dramatic effects. 'We are only now beginning to fulfil our proper potential and are reaching the dimensions programmed by our bodies,' says palaeontologist Professor Chris Stringer. 'We are becoming Cro-Magnons again – the people who lived on this planet 40,000 years ago.'

For most of human history, our ancestors got their food from a wide variety of sources: women gathered herbs, fruits and berries, while men supplemented these with occasional kills of animals (a way of life still adopted by the world's few remaining tribes of hunter-gatherers). **15** Then about 9,000 years ago, agriculture was invented – with devastating consequences. Most of the planet's green places have been gradually taken over by farmers, with the result that just three carbohydrate-rich plants – wheat, rice and maize – provide more than half of the calories consumed by the human race today.

16 Over the centuries we have lived on soups, porridges and breads that have left us underfed and underdeveloped. In one study of skeletons of American Indians in Ohio, scientists discovered that when they began to grow corn, healthy hunter-gatherers were turned into sickly, underweight farmers. Tooth decay increased, as did diseases. Far from being one of the blessings of the New World, corn was a public health disaster, according to some anthropologists.

17 The fact that most people relying on this system are poorly nourished and stunted has only recently been tackled, even by the world's wealthier nations. Only in Europe, the US and Japan are diets again reflecting the richness of our ancestors' diets.

As a result, the average man in the US is now 179cm, in Holland 180cm, and in Japan 177cm. It is a welcome trend, though not without its own problems. **18** A standard bed-length has remained at 190cm since 1860, while the height of a door was fixed at 198cm in 1880. Even worse, leg-room in planes and trains seems to have shrunk rather than grown, while clothes manufacturers are constantly having to revise their range of products.

The question is: where will it all end? We cannot grow for ever. **19** But what is it? According to Robert Fogel, of Chicago University, it could be as much as 193cm – and we are likely to reach it some time this century.

However, scientists add one note of qualification. Individuals may be growing taller because of improved nutrition, but as a species we are actually shrinking, although very slightly. During the last ice age, 10,000 years ago, members of the human race were slightly rounder and taller – an evolutionary response to the cold. (Large round bodies are best at keeping in heat.) **20** And as the planet continues to heat up, we may shrink even further. In other words, the growth of human beings could be offset by global warming.

A We must have some programmed upper limit.

B As they benefit from the changes in agriculture, people expect to have this wide variety of foods available.

C In fact, we are returning to what we were like as cavemen.

D This poor diet has had a disastrous effect on human health and physique.

E Since the climate warmed, we appear to have got slightly thinner and smaller, even when properly fed.

F Nevertheless, from then on agriculture spread because a piece of farmed land could support ten times the number of people who had previously lived off it as hunter-gatherers.

G One research study found that they based their diet on 85 different wild plants, for example.

H Heights may have risen, but the world has not moved on, it seems.

I Today, at 228cm, he is Britain's tallest man.

Part 4

You are going to read an article about guidebooks to London. For questions **21–35**, choose from the guidebooks (**A–G**). The guidebooks may be chosen more than once. When more than one answer is required, these may be given in any order. There is an example at the beginning (**0**).

Mark your answers **on the separate answer sheet**.

Of which guidebook(s) is the following stated?

It is frequently revised.	**0**	**F**
It is quite expensive.	**21**	
It is not aimed at local people.	**22**	
Its appearance is similar to other books by the same publisher.	**23**	
It contains some errors.	**24**	
It is reasonably priced.	**25**	
It shows great enthusiasm for the city.	**26**	
It has always been produced with a particular market in mind.	**27**	
It is written by people who have all the latest information.	**28**	
It is written in a friendly style.	**29**	**30**
It is part of the first series of its kind to be published.	**31**	
It omits some sights which should be included.	**32**	
It contains more information than other guides.	**33**	
It might appeal to London residents.	**34**	
Its information about places to eat is enjoyable to read.	**35**	

London Guidebooks

Visitors to London, which has so much to offer, need all the help they can get. Alastair Bickley takes his pick of the capital's guidebooks.

Guidebook A

Informal and familiar in tone, this valuable book has much to offer. Produced by the same people who put together London's principal listings magazine, this is right up to date with what's happening in the city – very much its home ground. It is concise enough to cater for those staying for just a couple of days, yet covers all areas of interest to visitors in an admirably condensed and approachable way. On balance, this is the single most handy book to have with you in London.

Guidebook B

This book is beautifully illustrated, with cutaway diagrams of buildings and bird's-eye-view itineraries rather than plain maps. This is a model of the clear professional design that is the recognisable trademark of this series. Its coverage of the main sights is strong, and visually it's a real treat – a delight to own as a practical guide. It's a bit pricey but well worth a look.

Guidebook C

Probably the best-suited for a longish stay in the city. This guide surpasses its competitors in its sheer depth of knowledge and in the detail it provides. It's particularly handy for the thorough stroller with plenty of time on his or her hands, covering virtually every building or monument of any interest – and with well-drawn maps of each area. Its coverage of all types of restaurants, which encourages you to go out and try them, can also be appreciated from the comfort of your armchair.

Guidebook D

In many ways, this serviceable guide is broadly comparable to the other guides but, whereas many of them feel as though they come from the 'inside', this feels geared towards visitors from elsewhere in the English-speaking world. It has its strengths, offering decent coverage of the sights, museums and inexpensive places to eat.

Guidebook E

It is astonishing – and perhaps the greatest tribute one can pay to London as a city – that it's possible to have a high-quality holiday there and scarcely spend anything on admission charges. In this guide, the obvious bargains (National Gallery, British Museum, etc.) are almost lost among an impressive range of places which cost nothing to visit. It should pay more attention to the numerous wonderful churches in the City of London but otherwise this is a must for the seriously budget-conscious or the Londoner who is looking for something different (like me). The book itself isn't quite free, but at £4.95, it's not far off it.

Guidebook F

This is the latest in the longest-standing series of budget guides and, unlike its competitors, it is still definitely aimed at young backpackers. Its description of the sights is less detailed than most and the accuracy of some of the information is surprisingly poor for such a regularly updated publication. However, it manages to cram in everything of significance, and is strongly weighted towards practicalities and entertainment.

Guidebook G

Here is a guide which comes with a distinct personality rather than following the style of the series to which it belongs. It is chatty, companionable, opinionated, crammed full of history and anecdotes as well as practical information. I can best describe the experience (for that's what it is) of reading this book as follows: imagine arriving in town and being taken in hand by a local who is determined to show you the best of everything and to give you the benefit of their considerable experience of a city for which they obviously hold a passion.

PAPER 2   WRITING (1 hour 30 minutes)

Part 1

You **must** answer this question.

---

1   Some British people are coming to your area and you have been asked to help organise the group's visit.

Read the extract from a letter you have received from Mrs Davidson, the leader of the group, and the notes you have made. Then write a letter to Mrs Davidson, using all your notes.

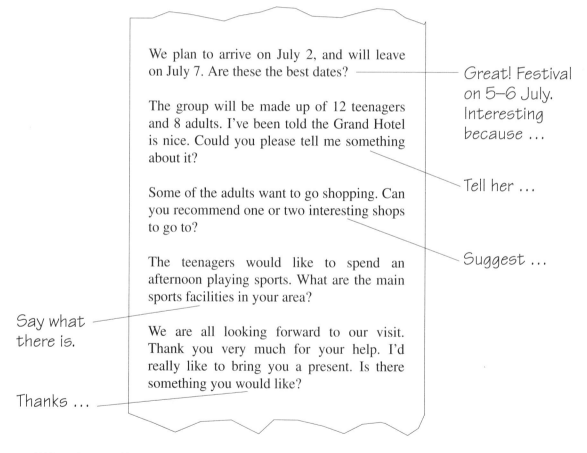

We plan to arrive on July 2, and will leave on July 7. Are these the best dates? — **Great! Festival on 5–6 July. Interesting because …**

The group will be made up of 12 teenagers and 8 adults. I've been told the Grand Hotel is nice. Could you please tell me something about it? — **Tell her …**

Some of the adults want to go shopping. Can you recommend one or two interesting shops to go to? — **Suggest …**

The teenagers would like to spend an afternoon playing sports. What are the main sports facilities in your area? — **Say what there is.**

We are all looking forward to our visit. Thank you very much for your help. I'd really like to bring you a present. Is there something you would like? — **Thanks …**

Write a **letter** of between **120** and **180** words in an appropriate style.
Do not write any postal addresses.

Part 2

Write an answer to **one** of the questions 2–5 in this part. Write your answer in **120–180** words in an appropriate style.

---

2   You have seen this announcement in an international music magazine.

> ## MUSIC ON THE RADIO
>
> Our readers tell us they love listening to music on the radio! What would your ideal evening music programme consist of? Write us an article:
> ● telling us what type of music you'd like to hear
> ● giving your suggestions for making the programme popular
> The writer with the best ideas will win £1,000 to spend on CDs.

Write your **article**.

3   You have had a class discussion on how people's lives will change in the future. Now your teacher has asked you to write a composition on the following statement:

People's lives will change dramatically in the next 50 years.

Write your **composition**.

4   An English friend, Jo, has written to you for some advice. This is part of the letter you have received.

> *I leave school this summer and have a year free before university. I want to come to your country. First I'd like to spend some time travelling. Then I'd like to find a job for three months. Please give me some advice on travelling and working in your country.*
>
> *Thanks, Jo*

Write your **letter**. Do not write any postal addresses.

5   Answer **one** of the following two questions based on your reading of **one** of these set books. Write **(a)** or **(b)** as well as the number **5** in the question box, and the **title** of the book next to the box. Your answer **must** be about one of the books below.

Best Detective Stories of Agatha Christie – Longman Fiction
A Tale of Two Cities – Charles Dickens
Animal Farm – George Orwell
More Tales from Shakespeare – Charles and Mary Lamb
Round the World in Eighty Days – Jules Verne

Either   **(a)**   'In a story, the places are often more important than the people.' How true is this of the book or one of the short stories you have read? Write a **composition** giving your opinions.

Or   **(b)**   You have agreed to write an **article** for your college magazine on the book you have read. Write about an important day for one of the characters in the book or one of the short stories you have read. You should also explain why this day was important for the character.

35

PAPER 3   USE OF ENGLISH (1 hour 15 minutes)

Part 1

For questions **1–15**, read the text below and decide which answer (**A, B, C** or **D**) best fits each space. There is an example at the beginning (**0**).

Mark your answers **on the separate answer sheet.**

Example:

0   A face   **B** outline   **C** surface   **D** top

0	A	B	C	D
	▬	▭	▭	▭

UNDER THE CITY STREETS

While skyscraper offices and elegant apartment blocks remain the public **(0)** ..... of most major cities, these cities also have a mass of secret tunnels and hidden pipes below **(1)** ..... which keep everything working. This other world exists beneath many of our greatest cities, forgotten or neglected by all but a tiny **(2)** ..... of engineers and historians.

For example, there are more than 150 kilometres of rivers under the streets of London. Most have been **(3)** ..... over and, sadly, all that **(4)** ..... is their names. Perhaps the greatest **(5)** ..... to the city is the River Fleet, a **(6)** ..... great river which previously had beautiful houses on its **(7)** ..... . It now goes underground in the north of the city and **(8)** ..... into the River Thames by Blackfriars Bridge.

The London Underground **(9)** ..... 1000 kilometres of underground railway track winding under the capital and more than 100 stations below street level. Along some underground railway **(10)** ..... , commuters can sometimes catch a **(11)** ..... glimpse of the platforms of more than forty closed stations which have been left under the city. **(12)** ..... some are used as film sets, most **(13)** ..... forgotten. Some have had their entrances on the street turned into restaurants and shops, but most entrances have been **(14)** ..... down. Interestingly, there is also a special underground Post Office railway that **(15)** ..... a link between east and west London postal centres.

1 **A** land   **B** ground   **C** soil   **D** earth

2 **A** number   **B** amount   **C** total   **D** few

3 **A** covered   **B** protected   **C** hidden   **D** sheltered

4 **A** stays   **B** stops   **C** remains   **D** keeps

5 **A** miss   **B** absence   **C** waste   **D** loss

6 **A** once   **B** past   **C** then   **D** prior

7 **A** borders   **B** coasts   **C** banks   **D** rims

8 **A** gets   **B** flows   **C** leaks   **D** lets

9 **A** holds   **B** contains   **C** has   **D** consists

10 **A** lanes   **B** avenues   **C** paths   **D** lines

11 **A** rapid   **B** brief   **C** fast   **D** sharp

12 **A** Despite   **B** Unless   **C** Although   **D** Since

13 **A** lie   **B** last   **C** live   **D** lay

14 **A** pulled   **B** broken   **C** brought   **D** cut

15 **A** occurs   **B** provides   **C** gives   **D** results

Part 2

For questions **16–30**, read the text below and think of the word which best fits each space. Use only **one** word in each space. There is an example at the beginning (**0**).

Write your answers **on the separate answer sheet**.

Example: | **0** | *the* |

MY HOME TOWN

I was born in one of **(0)** ....*the*.... most interesting cities in Malaysia. It has a rich, colourful history and many parts of the city have hardly changed at **(16)** .... during the last five centuries. However, nowadays, it is **(17)** .... longer the trade centre that it once **(18)** .... It is difficult to imagine that at one time its harbour **(19)** .... to be visited by over 2,000 ships a week, and that the huge warehouses along the quayside would have **(20)** .... full of spices and silks, jewels and tea.

The old city centre is small, which **(21)** .... it very easy to explore **(22)** .... foot. A river neatly divides the town, **(23)** .... only physically but in spirit too. On one side, you find a **(24)** .... many grand houses, but immediately you cross the river, you find **(25)** .... in ancient Chinatown, which is where you really **(26)** .... a step back into the past.

From the earliest times, this has been the heart of the city and it's fun to wander through the colourful, noisy backstreets. As **(27)** .... as the streets that sell a wide **(28)** .... of clothes and shoes, there are also streets famous **(29)** .... high quality antiques. Unfortunately, most of the bargains disappeared many years ago. However, **(30)** .... you look around carefully, you could still come across an interesting souvenir.

Part 3

For questions **31–40**, complete the second sentence so that it has a similar meaning to the first sentence, using the word given. **Do not change the word given.** You must use between **two** and **five** words, including the word given.

Here is an example (**0**).

Example:

0 A very friendly taxi driver drove us into town.

driven

We .... a very friendly taxi driver.

The space can be filled by the words 'were driven into town by' so you write:

0	*were driven into town by*

Write **only** the missing words on **the separate answer sheet**.

---

31 Nina's parents said she wasn't to use their new camera.

let

Nina's parents .... use their new camera.

32 The TV programme was so complicated that none of the children could understand it.

too

The TV programme was .... the children to understand.

33 The only shoes I could find to fit me were in black leather.

any

I could .... fitted me, apart from some in black leather.

34 Luke knocked over the old lady's bicycle by accident.

mean

Luke .... knock over the old lady's bicycle.

35 I've already planned my next holiday.

arrangements

I've already .... my next holiday.

36 They say the ice in Antarctica is getting thinner all the time.

said

The ice in Antarctica .... getting thinner all the time.

37 We didn't enjoy our walk along the seafront because it was so windy.

prevented

The strong wind .... our walk along the seafront.

38 It looks as if Susan has left her jacket behind.

seems

Susan .... her jacket behind.

39 A newly-qualified dentist took out Mr Dupont's tooth.

had

Mr Dupont .... by a newly-qualified dentist.

40 Antonio only lost the 100-metre race because he fell.

not

If Antonio had .... won the 100-metre race.

Part 4

For questions **41–55**, read the text below and look carefully at each line. Some of the lines are correct, and some have a word which should not be there.

If a line is correct, put a tick (✓) by the number **on the separate answer sheet**. If a line has a word which should **not** be there, write the word **on the separate answer sheet**. There are two examples at the beginning (**0** and **00**).

0	✓

Examples:

00	*nevertheless*

PLAYING CHESS

0	In your last letter you asked me to tell you why I like playing
00	chess so much. Well, I nevertheless think it is because chess gives
41	me a feeling of the excitement. I am quite competitive and like
42	the challenge of playing one-to-one. It gets intense sometimes;
43	in a game you can get extremely nervous and excited and have all
44	sorts of emotions. If I have played such a good player, put up
45	a good fight and lost, then that is too satisfying, but it is always
46	better than to win! There is also a good social side to chess. I
47	have made lots of friends at playing in competitions across
48	Europe. It is really interesting seeing cultures more different from
49	mine and trying to practise other languages! Now I play most of
50	weekends and holidays, but I do not know for certain if I will continue
51	to take part in competitions. During the last couple of years while I
52	have had more schoolwork, in which makes life more difficult. You
53	have got to be an extremely good player for chess to be so financially
54	worthwhile. However, I would like recommend it as a hobby to
55	anyone. If you are interested, you should to join a chess club at once.

Part 5

For questions **56–65**, read the text below. Use the word given in capitals at the end of each line to form a word that fits in the space in the **same** line. There is an example at the beginning (**0**).

Write your answers **on the separate answer sheet**.

Example: | **0** | *existence* |

BIGFOOT

There are some people who believe in the (**0**) ....*existence*.... of Bigfoot,   **EXIST**

a (**56**) .... ape-like creature that is supposed to live in the mountains   **MYSTERY**

of the USA. In 1967, some hunters claimed to have (**57**) .... filmed   **ACCIDENT**

such a creature and many people see this as firm (**58**) .... that   **PROVE**

Bigfoot is real.

But now, researchers have come to the (**59**) .... that the film is a trick.   **CONCLUDE**

After a close (**60**) .... of it, they claim to have identified a man-made   **ANALYSE**

fastener at the creature's waist. Bigfoot is, therefore, (**61**) .... to be   **LIKELY**

anything more than a man in an animal suit.

Some people remain unconvinced by the (**62**) .... , though. Bigfoot fans   **SCIENCE**

are extremely (**63**) .... that a fastener would show up on such an old film.   **DOUBT**

In (**64**) .... , they say that the creature caught on camera does not move   **ADD**

like a human and that it is therefore (**65**) .... a wild creature of nature.   **TRUE**

The debate goes on.

Visual materials for Paper 5

1A

1B

1E

1C

1D

2A

2B

2E

2C

2D

3A

3B

3E

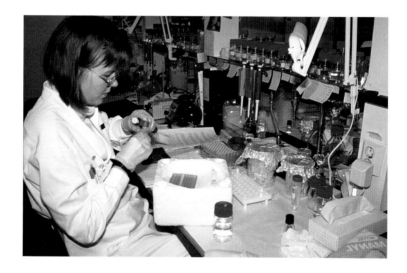

3C

3D

4A

4B

4E

4C

4D

PAPER 4   LISTENING (approximately 40 minutes)

Part 1

You will hear people talking in eight different situations. For questions **1–8**, choose the best answer (**A**, **B** or **C**).

---

1   You hear part of an interview in which a film director talks about his favourite movie.
Why does he like the film?

   A   It is very funny.

   B   It is very exciting.

   C   It is very romantic.

	1

2   You hear a man talking about a sofa he bought.
What is he complaining about?

   A   He received the wrong sofa.

   B   The shop overcharged him for the sofa.

   C   The sofa was damaged.

	2

3   You hear an actor talking about using different accents in his work.
What point is he making about actors?

   A   They need to study a wide variety of accents.

   B   They have to be able to control their use of accents.

   C   They should try to keep their original accents.

	3

4   You hear part of an interview in which a man is talking about winning his first horse race.
What does he say about it?

   A   He found it rather disappointing.

   B   He didn't have a chance to celebrate.

   C   He was too tired to care.

	4

5 You hear a writer of musicals talking on the radio.
What is he trying to explain?

    A   why his aunt's career was not very successful

    B   the difference between American and British musicals

    C   his reasons for becoming a writer of musicals

5

6 You hear the beginning of a lecture about ancient history.
What is the lecture going to be about?

    A   trade in arms and weapons

    B   trade in luxury household goods

    C   trade in works of art

6

7 You hear a man talking about travelling from London to France for his job.
What does he say about the train journey?

    A   He's able to use it to his advantage.

    B   It's a boring but necessary part of his job.

    C   He enjoys the social aspect of it.

7

8 You hear a woman in a shop talking about some lost photographs.
What does she think the shop should give her?

    A   some money

    B   a replacement film

    C   an apology

8

Part 2

You will hear part of a radio interview with a woman who sailed round the world on her own. For questions **9–18**, complete the sentences.

Anna was employed by a [**9**] when she first started sailing.

The idea of sailing round the world came from a book called [**10**]

Anna spent some time [**11**] the boat before taking it out to sea.

Anna tested her boat on a trip which lasted for only [**12**] because it was damaged.

Anna got the money she needed to make the trip from various [**13**] companies.

Anna's worst problem during the trip was when she felt [**14**] because the boat was going so slowly.

Anna found the [**15**] in the Southern Ocean the most exciting part of the trip.

On her return, Anna phoned the [**16**] to ask for a certificate.

Anna's claim was doubted because she hadn't been in contact with people on [**17**] during her trip.

Anna's story was finally believed after her [**18**] had been checked.

Part 3

You will hear five young people talking about what makes a good teacher. For questions **19–23**, choose from the list (**A–F**) which of the opinions each speaker expresses. Use the letters only once. There is one extra letter which you do not need to use.

A A good teacher praises effort.

	19

Speaker 1

B A good teacher knows the subject well.

	20

Speaker 2

C A good teacher is strict.

	21

Speaker 3

D A good teacher is available outside the classroom.

	22

Speaker 4

E A good teacher is entertaining.

	23

Speaker 5

F A good teacher has experience.

Part 4

You will hear a radio interview about a mountain-climbing weekend. For questions **24–30**, choose the best answer (**A**, **B** or **C**).

24 How did Douglas feel when he booked the weekend?

   A   sure that he would enjoy training for it

   B   uncertain if it was a good idea for him

   C   surprised that such activities were organised

	24

25 Douglas expected that the experience would help him to

   A   meet people with similar interests.

   B   improve his physical fitness.

   C   discover his psychological limits.

	25

26 He was surprised that the other participants

   A   were there for reasons like his.

   B   were experienced climbers.

   C   were in better condition than him.

	26

27 What did one of his friends say to him?

   A   He was making a mistake.

   B   Climbing was fashionable.

   C   She was envious of him.

	27

28 What did the people plan at the end of the trip?

   A   to send each other postcards

   B   to take a different sort of trip together

   C   to go on another climbing trip together

	28

29 In what way did Douglas change as a result of the trip?

   A   He developed more interest in people.

   B   He became more ambitious.

   C   He began to notice more things around him.

	29

30 Douglas's boots are still muddy because he wants them to

   A   remind him of what he has achieved.

   B   warn him not to do it again.

   C   show other people what he has done.

	30

PAPER 5   SPEAKING (14 minutes)

You take the Speaking test with another candidate, referred to here as your partner. There are two examiners. One will speak to you and your partner and the other will be listening. Both examiners will award marks.

Part 1 (3 minutes)

The examiner asks you and your partner questions about yourselves. You may be asked about things like 'your home town', 'your interests', 'your career plans', etc.

Part 2 (4 minutes)

The examiner gives you two photographs and asks you to talk about them for one minute. The examiner then asks your partner a question about your photographs and your partner responds briefly.

Then the examiner gives your partner two different photographs. Your partner talks about these photographs for one minute. This time the examiner asks you a question about your partner's photographs and you respond briefly.

Part 3 (approximately 3 minutes)

The examiner asks you and your partner to talk together. You may be asked to solve a problem or try to come to a decision about something. For example, you might be asked to decide the best way to use some rooms in a language school. The examiner gives you a picture to help you but does not join in the conversation.

Part 4 (approximately 4 minutes)

The examiner joins in the conversation. You all talk together in a more general way about what has been said in Part 3. The examiner asks you questions but you and your partner are also expected to develop the conversation.

Test 3

PAPER 1   READING (1 hour 15 minutes)

Part 1

You are going to read a magazine article about the popularity of activity holidays. Choose the most suitable heading from the list **A–I** for each part (**1–7**) of the article. There is one extra heading which you do not need to use. There is an example at the beginning (**0**).

Mark your answers **on the separate answer sheet**.

A	A false sense of security
B	Remote destinations
C	Too risky for some
D	Holidays that don't quite work
E	New findings
F	Very little real danger
G	Too much routine
H	Second-hand experiences
I	Available to all

Activity Holidays

Whether it's bungee-jumping, climbing or sky-diving, we want to test ourselves on holiday. Peter Jones tries to find out why.

0	I

Risk-taking for pleasure is on the increase. Adventure activities and 'extreme' sports are becoming very popular and attracting everyone from the young and fit to people who, until recently, were more likely to prefer walking round museums at weekends. Grandmothers are white-water rafting, secretaries are bungee-jumping, and accountants are climbing cliffs.

1	

Well-planned summer expeditions to tropical locations are now fashionable for European university students. As they wander over ancient rocks or canoe past tiny villages, away from it all, it is quite possible to feel 'in tune with nature', a real explorer or adventurer.

2	

A whole branch of the travel industry is now developing around controlled risks. Ordinary trippers, too, are met off a plane, strapped into rafts or boats and are given the sort of adventure that they will remember for years. They pay their money and they trust their guides, and the wetter they get the better. Later, they buy the photograph of themselves 'risking all in the wild'.

3	

But why the fashion for taking risks, real or simulated? The point that most people make is that city life is tame, with little variety, and increasingly controlled. Physical exercise is usually restricted to aerobics in the gym on a Thursday, and a game of football or tennis in the park or a short walk at the weekend.

4	

Says Trish Malcolm, an independent tour operator: 'People want a sense of immediate achievement and the social element of shared physical experience is also important.' Other operators say that people find the usual type of breaks – such as a week on the beach – too slow. They say that participation in risk sports is a reflection of the restlessness in people. They are always on the go in their lives and want to keep up the momentum on holiday.

5	

But psychologists think it's even deeper than this. Culturally, we are being separated from the physical, outside world. Recent research suggests that the average person spends less and less time out of doors per day.

6	

Nature and the great outdoors are mostly encountered through wildlife films or cinema, or seen rushing past the windows of a fast car. In a society where people are continually invited to watch rather than to participate, a two-hour ride down a wild and fast-flowing river can be incredibly exciting.

7	

One psychologist believes that it is all part of our need to control nature. Because we have developed the technology to make unsinkable boats, boots that can stop us getting frostbite or jackets that allow us to survive in extreme temperatures, we are beginning to believe that nothing will harm us and that we are protected from nature. That is until nature shows us her true power in the form of a storm, flood or avalanche.

Part 2

You are going to read a magazine article in which a father describes his relationship with his son. For questions **8–14**, choose the answer (**A**, **B**, **C** or **D**) which you think fits best according to the text.

Mark your answers **on the separate answer sheet**.

Gary and Me

The restaurant owner John Moore writes about his relationship with his son Gary, the famous TV chef.

I believe everyone's given a chance in life. My son, Gary, was given his chance with cooking, and my chance was to run a restaurant. When I heard about the opportunity, I rushed over to look at the place. It was in a really bad state. It was perfect for what I had in mind.

Coming into this business made me recall my childhood. I can remember my mother going out to work in a factory and me being so upset because I was left alone. With that in mind, I thought, 'We want time for family life'. My wife dedicated herself to looking after the children and did all my accounts while I ran the business. We lived over the restaurant in those days, and we always put a lot of emphasis on having meals *line 16* together. It's paid dividends with our children, Gary and Joe. They're both very confident. Also, from a very early age they would come down and talk to our regular customers. It's given both of them a great start in life.

Gary was quite a lively child when he was really small. We had a corner bath, and when he was about seven he thought he'd jump into it like a swimming pool, and he knocked himself out. When he was older, he had to work for pocket money. He started off doing odd jobs and by the age of about ten he was in the kitchen every weekend, so he always had loads of money at school. He had discipline. He used to be up even before me in the morning. If you run a family business, it's for the family, and it was nice to see him helping out.

Gary wasn't very academic, but he shone so much in the kitchen. By the age of fifteen he was as good as any of the men working there, and sometimes he was even left in charge. He would produce over a hundred meals, and from then I knew he'd go into catering because he had that flair. So when he came to me and said, 'Dad, I've got to do work experience as part of my course at school', I sent him to a friend of mine who's got a restaurant.

Gary recently took up playing the drums and now he has his own band. Goodness knows what will happen to the cooking if the music takes off. My advice to Gary would be: if you start chasing two hares, you end up catching neither, so chase the hare you know you're going to catch. He understood when I said to him: 'Gary, if you're going to get anywhere in life, you've got to do it by the age of 30. If you haven't done it by then, it's too late.' *line 52*

Gary went to catering college at the age of 17, and on his first day he and the other new students – they're normally complete beginners – were given what's supposed to be a morning's work. But within an hour, Gary had chopped all his vegetables, sliced all his meats. He'd prepared everything. That's my son for you! In the end, he was helping other people out.

None of us can believe how successful Gary's TV cookery series has become. I'm extremely proud of him. I've always tried to tell him that if you want something, you've got to work jolly hard for it, because no one gives you anything. He's seen the opportunity he's been given and grabbed hold of it with both hands. You know, you talk to your children as they grow up, and if they only take in ten per cent of what you've told them, you've got to be happy with that. The things Gary says, the things he does, I think, well, he must have listened sometimes.

8 How did the writer react to his own big chance?

    A He worried about the problems.

    B He saw what could be done.

    C He thought the family would suffer.

    D He wondered if he should take it.

9 How did the writer's childhood influence his own family life?

    A He realised that the pattern was repeating itself.

    B He encouraged his children to talk to him.

    C He made sure there was plenty of personal contact.

    D He forced his wife to stay at home.

10 What does the writer mean by 'paid dividends' in line 16?

    A brought financial reward

    B produced benefits

    C was worth the suffering

    D allowed money to be saved

11 As a young boy, Gary

    A showed how determined he could be.

    B was always in trouble.

    C was motivated by money.

    D demonstrated a variety of talents.

12 What does 'done it' refer to in line 52?

    A chosen a profession

    B achieved success

    C caught a hare

    D lived your life

13 According to his father, what was typical about Gary's behaviour on his first day at college?

    A He helped other people.

    B He impressed those in charge.

    C He tried to make his father proud.

    D He performed the task efficiently.

14 How does his father regard Gary's upbringing?

    A His encouragement has caused Gary's success.

    B The family influence on Gary was too strong.

    C Gary has forgotten important lessons.

    D Gary has learnt some essential things.

Part 3

You are going to read a magazine article about learning to fly a plane. Eight paragraphs have been removed from the article. Choose from the paragraphs **A–I** the one which fits each gap (**15–21**). There is one extra paragraph which you do not need to use. There is an example at the beginning (**0**).

Mark your answers **on the separate answer sheet**.

Learning to Fly

I had been testing cars and motorcycles for over twenty years. I couldn't take any more. It wasn't terribly exciting and, in any case, new cars were beginning to look identical and drive similarly. What I needed was a new challenge.

0	I

Unfortunately, I wore glasses. The Royal Air Force wouldn't consider anyone for pilot training unless they had perfect eyesight. Halfway through an aptitude test, they realised that my eyes were far from perfect. I didn't stand a chance.

15	

It was an obvious choice. It's just twenty minutes' drive from my home. It's very quiet, too, so the £90 per hour for the training is spent flying in the air, not waiting on the ground for other planes to take off.

16	

It took me a whole year to get my private pilot's licence. It started well, with my first solo flight coming after just seven hours. Then came all the studying, the exams, the hard work. I never thought I'd get to the end of it.

17	

Then came last winter and the end of the course was in sight. For weeks, the weather was so terrible that for most of the time it was impossible to fly. Strong winds, heavy rain and even snow and ice made flying conditions extremely hazardous.

18	

But finally the first of three practical exams arrived – the navigation test. The examiner sets you a course that you have to plan according to the weather, and then fly with him sitting beside you.

19	

I passed this test, but I don't know how. The second test involves flying cross-country to two other airports, which you can choose, and landing at both. The important thing is to give the right messages to the air-traffic control people and understand their replies.

20	

After this alarming episode, the exercises in the flight-handling test were simple. As we completed the sixth exercise, the examiner suddenly turned to me and said, 'Congratulations – you've passed!'

21	

I wasn't sure why, because we usually land as slowly as possible. Then I turned round and realised straightaway: we were being followed by a British Airways jumbo jet!

A   A week which I had set aside for finishing the course came and went with no possibility of getting in the air at all. And besides the problems with the weather, my second son was born, and that made it even more difficult to find the time for lessons and studying.

B   But the real reason I chose this club was that a friend of mine, Andrew Wilkins, is the chief instructor there. He impressed me by taking me out for a free flight just so that I could see what it was like.

C   Unfortunately, I got myself lost this time and flew too far east. I completely missed the first airport. However, I flew over a car factory I recognised and managed to get back on course.

D   Along the way, he'll take the controls and fly off course, just to get you lost. Then he'll hand back the controls to you and expect you to find your way home.

E   One day I was asked by an air-traffic controller if I could see another aircraft ahead. I said yes, and immediately it disappeared into a cloud. I just didn't know what to do.

F   At the time, taking private lessons to learn how to fly was financially beyond me. So I had to delay my plans to become a pilot for quite a while. It was twenty years, in fact, before I finally enrolled at a flying club in Hertfordshire.

G   Since getting my pilot's licence, I've been out flying a few times. The highlight so far was flying up to Birmingham International Airport for a motor show with Andrew beside me. As we approached the runway, the air-traffic controller came on the radio asking for as much speed as our little plane could manage.

H   For months, my head was always in a book and my head hurt from all the facts, figures and flying instructions.

I   This feeling of needing a change coincided with my 40th birthday, which started me thinking about what I'd been doing all those years. When I left school all I had really wanted to do was fly.

Part 4

You are going to read an article about the effect of advertising on children. For questions **22–35**, choose from the sections of the article (**A–F**). The sections may be chosen more than once. There is an example at the beginning (**0**).

Mark your answers **on the separate answer sheet**.

Which section of the article mentions

the kind of shop in which TV advertising expects to see results?	**0**	**B**
the influence a parent has had over their child's views?	**22**	
the fact that children do not understand why their parents refuse their demands?	**23**	
a parent who understands why children make demands?	**24**	
a family who rarely argue while shopping?	**25**	
someone who feels children ought to find out for themselves how to make decisions about what to buy?	**26**	
the fact that parents can be mistaken about what food is good for you?	**27**	
an unexpected benefit for shops?	**28**	
a parent who regrets buying what their children have asked for?	**29**	
a parent who has different rules for themselves and their children?	**30**	
a parent who feels annoyed even before the children ask for anything?	**31**	
the fact that parents blame the advertisers for the difficult situation they find themselves in?	**32**	
the regularity of children's demands?	**33**	
the need for parents to discuss food with their children?	**34**	
a TV advertising rule which has little effect?	**35**	

Young Shoppers

A Supermarket shopping with children, one mother says, is absolute murder: 'They want everything they see. If it's not the latest sugar-coated breakfast cereal, it's a Disney video or a comic. Usually all three. I can't afford all this stuff and, anyway, if I agree to their demands I feel I've been persuaded against my better judgement and I feel guilty about buying and feeding them rubbish. Yet I hate myself for saying no all the time, and I get cross and defensive in anticipation as we leave home. I do my best to avoid taking them shopping but then I worry that I'm not allowing them to have the experience they need in order to make their own choices. I can't win.'

B Research has found that children taken on a supermarket trip make a purchase request every two minutes. More than £150 million a year is now spent on advertising directly to children, most of it on television. That figure is likely to increase and it is in the supermarket aisles that the investment is most likely to be successful. For children, the reasons behind their parents' decisions about what they can and cannot afford are often unclear, and arguments about how bad sugar is for your teeth are unconvincing when compared with the attractive and emotionally persuasive advertising campaigns.

C According to Susan Dibb of the National Food Alliance, 'Most parents are concerned about what they give their children to eat and have ideas about what food is healthy – although those ideas are not always accurate. Obviously, such a dialogue between parents and children is a good thing, because if the only information children are getting about products is from TV advertising, they are getting a very one-sided view. Parents resent the fact that they are competing with the advertising industry and are forced into the position of repeatedly disappointing their children.' The Independent Television Commission, which regulates TV advertising, prohibits advertisers from telling children to ask their parents to buy products. But, as

Dibb points out, 'The whole purpose of advertising is to persuade the viewer to buy something. So even if they cannot say, "Tell your mum to buy this product," the intended effect is precisely that.'

D A major source of stress for some parents shopping with children is the mental energy required to decide which demands should be agreed to and which should be refused. One mother says she has patience when it comes to discussing food with her children, but she still feels unhappy about the way she manages their shopping demands: 'My son does pay attention to advertisements but he is critical of them. We talk a lot about different products and spend time looking at labels. I've talked about it so much that I've brainwashed him into thinking all adverts are rubbish. We have very little conflict in the supermarket now because the children don't ask for things I won't want to buy.'

E Parents also admit they are inconsistent, even hypocritical, in their responses to their children's purchasing requests. Mike, father of a son of seven and a daughter of three, says, 'We refuse to buy him the sweets he wants on the grounds that it's bad for him while we are busy loading the trolley with double cream and chocolate for ourselves. It's enjoyable to buy nice things, and it's quite reasonable that children should want to share that, I suppose. But I still find myself being irritated by their demands. It partly depends on how I feel. If I'm feeling generous and things are going well in my life, I'm more likely to say yes. It's hard to be consistent.'

F Supermarkets themselves could do a lot more to ease parent-child conflict by removing sweets from checkout areas or even by providing supervised play areas. Although parents might spend less without their children with them, the thought of shopping without your six-year-old's demands would surely attract enough extra customers to more than make up the difference.

PAPER 2   WRITING (1 hour 30 minutes)

Part 1

You **must** answer this question.

1   An English friend, Sam, visited you recently and has just sent you a letter and some photographs. Read Sam's letter and the notes you have made on it. Then write a suitable letter to Sam, using all your notes.

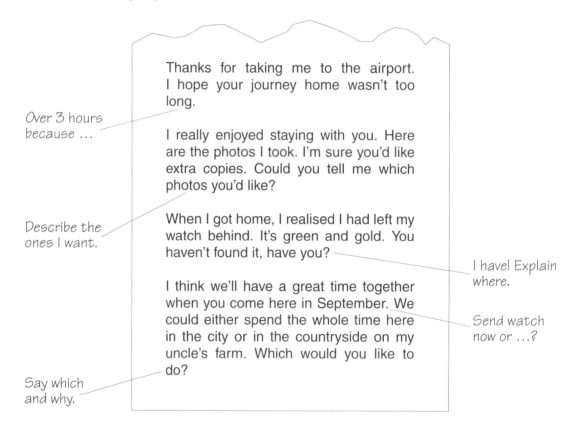

Over 3 hours because …

Thanks for taking me to the airport. I hope your journey home wasn't too long.

I really enjoyed staying with you. Here are the photos I took. I'm sure you'd like extra copies. Could you tell me which photos you'd like?

Describe the ones I want.

When I got home, I realised I had left my watch behind. It's green and gold. You haven't found it, have you?

I have! Explain where.

I think we'll have a great time together when you come here in September. We could either spend the whole time here in the city or in the countryside on my uncle's farm. Which would you like to do?

Send watch now or …?

Say which and why.

Write a **letter** of between **120** and **180** words in an appropriate style.
Do not write any postal addresses.

Part 2

Write an answer to **one** of the questions **2–5** in this part. Write your answer in **120–180** words in an appropriate style.

---

2   Your teacher has asked you to write a composition, giving your opinions on the following statement:

Your teenage years are the best years of your life!

Write your **composition**.

3   You see the following notice in an international magazine.

> # Be someone famous for a day
>
> If you could change places for 24 hours with a famous person alive today, who would you choose, and why?
>
> The best article will be published in our magazine next month.

Write your **article**.

4   You have decided to enter a short story competition in an international magazine. The competition rules say that the story must **end** with the following words:

That one telephone call changed my life for ever.

Write your **story**.

5   Answer **one** of the following two questions based on your reading of **one** of these set books. Write **(a)** or **(b)** as well as the number **5** in the question box, and the **title** of the book next to the box. Your answer **must** be about one of the books below.

Best Detective Stories of Agatha Christie – Longman Fiction
A Tale of Two Cities – Charles Dickens
Animal Farm – George Orwell
More Tales from Shakespeare – Charles and Mary Lamb
Round the World in Eighty Days – Jules Verne

Either   **(a)**   In the story you have read, which character would you most like to be? Write a **composition** for your teacher, answering this question with reference to the book or one of the short stories you have read.

Or   **(b)**   'A love story is an essential part of every good book.' Do you agree or disagree with this statement? Write a **composition**, giving your opinions with reference to the book or one of the short stories you have read.

PAPER 3 USE OF ENGLISH (1 hour 15 minutes)

Part 1

For questions **1–15**, read the text below and decide which answer (**A**, **B**, **C** or **D**) best fits each space. There is an example at the beginning (**0**).

Mark your answers **on the separate answer sheet.**

Example:

0 **A** catch   **B** pick   **C** find   **D** gain

0	A	B	C	D
	▬	⬭	⬭	⬭

A GOOD START TO A HOLIDAY

I had never been to Denmark before, so when I set out to **(0)** ..... the ferry in early May, I little **(1)** ..... that by the end of the trip I'd have made such lasting friendships.

Esjberg is a **(2)** ..... port for a cyclist's arrival, where tourist information can be **(3)** ..... and money changed. A cycle track **(4)** ..... out of town and down to Ribe, where I spent my first night. The only appointment I had to **(5)** ..... was a meeting with a friend who was flying out in June. I wanted to **(6)** ..... my time well, so I had planned a route which would **(7)** ..... several small islands and various **(8)** ..... of the countryside.

In my **(9)** ..... , a person travelling alone sometimes meets with unexpected hospitality, and this trip was no **(10)** ..... . On only my second day, I got into conversation with a cheerful man who turned **(11)** ..... to be the local baker. He insisted that I should **(12)** ..... his family for lunch, and, while we were eating, he contacted his daughter in Odense. Within minutes, he had **(13)** ..... for me to visit her and her family. Then I was **(14)** ..... on my way with a fresh loaf of bread to keep me **(15)** ..... , and the feeling that this would turn out to be a wonderful holiday.

1 **A** wondered   **B** suspected   **C** doubted   **D** judged

2 **A** capable   **B** ready   **C** favourable   **D** convenient

3 **A** met   **B** united   **C** established   **D** obtained

4 **A** leads   **B** rides   **C** moves   **D** connects

5 **A** do   **B** support   **C** keep   **D** maintain

6 **A** take   **B** serve   **C** exercise   **D** use

7 **A** include   **B** contain   **C** enclose   **D** consist

8 **A** sectors   **B** parts   **C** zones   **D** places

9 **A** experience   **B** knowledge   **C** observation   **D** information

10 **A** difference   **B** change   **C** exception   **D** contrast

11 **A** up   **B** out   **C** in   **D** over

12 **A** greet   **B** see   **C** join   **D** approach

13 **A** arranged   **B** fixed   **C** settled   **D** ordered

14 **A** passed   **B** sent   **C** begun   **D** put

15 **A** doing   **B** making   **C** being   **D** going

Part 2

For questions **16–30**, read the text below and think of the word which best fits each space. Use only **one** word in each space. There is an example at the beginning (**0**).

Write your answers **on the separate answer sheet**.

Example: | **0** | *away* |

DEALING WITH WASTE PLASTIC

Every year people throw (**0**) ...*away*... millions of tonnes of plastic bottles, boxes and wrapping. These create huge mountains of waste (**16**) .... are extremely hard to get (**17**) .... of. Now, a new recycling process promises to reduce this problem by turning old plastic (**18**) .... new.

Scientists have taken (**19**) .... long time to develop their ideas because waste plastic has always been a bigger problem (**20**) .... substances like waste paper. You can bury plastic, but it is years (**21**) .... it breaks down. If you burn it, it just becomes another form of pollution. A (**22**) .... products, for example bottles, can be re-used but it is expensive or difficult to do this (**23**) .... a lot of plastic products.

Now a group of companies has developed a new method (**24**) .... recycling that could save almost (**25**) .... plastic waste. The advantage of the new process is that nearly every type of waste plastic can be used: it does (**26**) .... have to be sorted. In addition, labels and ink may be left (**27**) .... the products. Everything is simply mixed together (**28**) .... heated to more than 400 degrees centigrade (**29**) .... that it melts. It is then cooled, producing a waxy substance that can be used to make new plastic products such as bags, bottles and, among (**30**) .... things, computer hardware.

Part 3

For questions **31–40**, complete the second sentence so that it has a similar meaning to the first sentence, using the word given. **Do not change the word given**. You must use between **two** and **five** words, including the word given.

Here is an example (**0**).

Example:

0 You must do exactly what the manager tells you.

carry

You must .... instructions exactly.

The space can be filled by the words 'carry out the manager's' so you write:

0	*carry out the manager's*

Write **only** the missing words on **the separate answer sheet**.

_____

31 The teacher postponed the theatre trip until the summer term.

off

The theatre trip .... the teacher until the summer term.

32 'What is the width of this cupboard?' Rebecca asked her sister.

wide

Rebecca asked her sister .... was.

33 George spent ages tidying up his room.

took

It .... up his room.

34 Claire accidentally damaged my book.

mean

Claire .... my book.

35   A famous architect designed Dr Schneider's house for her.

had

Dr Schneider .... a famous architect.

36   'Peter, you've eaten all the ice-cream!' said his mother.

accused

Peter's mother .... all the ice-cream.

37   Jim fell off his bike because he wasn't looking where he was going.

paying

If Jim .... to where he was going, he wouldn't have fallen off his bike.

38   Maria apologised for breaking Sarah's camera.

sorry

Maria said she .... broken Sarah's camera.

39   We might not find it easy to book a seat at the last minute.

could

It .... us to book a seat at the last minute.

40   It was wrong of you to borrow my jacket without asking.

ought

You .... before you borrowed my jacket.

Part 4

For questions **41–55**, read the text below and look carefully at each line. Some of the lines are correct, and some have a word which should not be there.

If a line is correct, put a tick (✓) by the number **on the separate answer sheet**. If a line has a word which should **not** be there, write the word **on the separate answer sheet**. There are two examples at the beginning (**0** and **00**).

0	✓

Examples:

00	*with*

THE PAINTING

0	In the village where I grew up, everyone knew an old man
00	who spent all of his time with painting. People who lived in the
41	village used to be admire his work and he often gave paintings
42	to friends of his. If they offered him money, he would never
43	take it because he said he painted for a pleasure. He gave one of
44	the paintings to my father, who actually wasn't very interested
45	in art. One day when I was playing, I came across from it in the
46	bin outside our house. I have hid it in our garage where my father
47	couldn't find it because I really would liked it, and then I forgot
48	all about it. Since years later I found it again. By that time the
49	old man had been died and people had started to recognise his
50	paintings as great works of art. They were now worth a lot of
51	money. An art gallery made me an offer of £5,000 for this
52	painting and I nearly sold it, but then I decided not to do. When
53	I look at the painting held hanging on the wall of my sitting-room,
54	it reminds to me of my childhood, and of the man who could
55	have been so much rich but didn't really want to make money.

Part 5

For questions **56–65**, read the text below. Use the word given in capitals at the end of each line to form a word that fits in the space in the **same** line. There is an example at the beginning (**0**).

Write your answers **on the separate answer sheet**.

Example:

0	*cheerfully*

AN UNUSUAL SWIMMING CLUB

Members of a special club in Britain (**0**) ....*cheerfully*.... leave the warmth   **CHEER**

of their beds, while most sensible people are still fast (**56**) .... , for   **SLEEP**

an (**57**) .... swim in water with a temperature of only seven degrees   **ENERGY**

centigrade. This may sound like (**58**) .... to you, but these swimmers   **MAD**

firmly believe that it is (**59**) .... to do this, even in mid-winter.   **HEALTH**

(**60**) .... of the club requires daily swimming outdoors. However,   **MEMBER**

for people not used to large (**61**) .... in temperature,   **DIFFERENT**

it may not be such a good idea. While there is an (**62**) .... in   **IMPROVE**

the blood circulation of people who swim (**63**) .... in icy water,   **REGULAR**

it can be (**64**) .... to others. But when members are asked why they   **HARM**

do it, the common (**65**) .... is that it makes them feel wonderful!   **RESPOND**

PAPER 4   LISTENING (approximately 40 minutes)

Part 1

You will hear people talking in eight different situations. For questions **1–8**, choose the best answer (**A**, **B** or **C**).

1   You hear a man talking to a group of people who are going on an expedition
into the rainforest.
What does he advise them against?

   A   sleeping in places where insects are found

   B   using substances which attract insects

   C   bathing in areas where insects are common

	1

2   You overhear two people talking about a school football competition.
What did the woman think of the event?

   A   She didn't think anyone had enjoyed it.

   B   It managed to fulfil its aims.

   C   Not enough people had helped to set it up.

	2

3   You hear a woman talking about her studies at the Beijing Opera School.
How did she feel when she first started her classes?

   A   worried about being much older than the other students

   B   disappointed because her dictionary was unhelpful

   C   annoyed by the lack of communication with her teacher

	3

4   You hear a famous comedian talking on the radio about his early career.
Why is he telling this story?

   A   to show how lucky he was at the beginning

   B   to show the value of a good course

   C   to show that he has always been a good comedian

	4

5 You hear someone talking on the phone.
Who is she talking to?

    A someone at her office

    B someone at a travel information centre

    C a family member

      5

6 You hear a novelist talking about how she writes.
How does she get her ideas for her novels?

    A She bases her novels on personal experiences.

    B Ideas come to her once she starts writing.

    C She lets ideas develop gradually in her mind.

      6

7 You hear a woman talking to a friend on the phone.
What is she doing?

    A refusing an invitation

    B denying an accusation

    C apologising for a mistake

      7

8 You hear a radio announcement about a future programme.
What kind of programme is it?

    A a play about a child

    B a reading from a children's book

    C a holiday programme

      8

Part 2

You will hear an interview with a man who enjoys flying in a small aircraft called a 'microlight'.
For questions **9–18**, complete the sentences.

Before his retirement, Brian worked as a pilot for a company called

| | **9** | for a long time.

Brian feels like a bird when flying his microlight because he doesn't have a

| | **10** | around him.

Brian disagrees with the suggestion that steering a microlight is like steering a

| | **11** |

Brian's record-breaking flight ended in | | **12** |

Brian organised his flight in advance to avoid needing other people as

| | **13** | on the way.

Brian's microlight was modified so that it could carry more

| | **14** | on board.

It took Brian | | **15** | to plan the record-breaking flight.

Brian feels that flying over miles and miles of

| | **16** | was the most dangerous part of the trip.

Brian describes his navigation system as both

| | **17** | and easy to use.

Brian says that his main problem on the flight was the fact that he became very

| | **18** |

Part 3

You will hear five different people talking about short courses they have attended. For questions **19–23**, choose from the list (**A–F**) what each speaker says about their course. Use the letters only once. There is one extra letter which you do not need to use.

A I was encouraged by the teachers to continue developing my skill.

Speaker 1 [ ] **19**

B I learnt something about the subject that I hadn't expected.

Speaker 2 [ ] **20**

C I preferred the social life to the course content.

Speaker 3 [ ] **21**

D I intend doing a similar course again.

Speaker 4 [ ] **22**

E I found out something about myself.

Speaker 5 [ ] **23**

F I thought the course was good value for money.

Part 4

You will hear part of a radio interview with Martin Middleton, who makes wildlife programmes for television. For questions **24–30**, choose the best answer (**A**, **B** or **C**).

24 What was the origin of Martin Middleton's love of travel?

    A   living abroad in the 1960s

    B   something he read as a child

    C   a television film about Africa

               24

25 When he visited Borneo, Martin

    A   had no fixed expectations.

    B   made a programme about life on the river.

    C   became more interested in filming old buildings.

               25

26 Since the early 1960s, wildlife filming has become

    A   more relaxed.

    B   more creative.

    C   more organised.

               26

27 Looking back, Martin regards his experience on the iceberg as

    A   slightly ridiculous.

    B   extremely dangerous.

    C   strangely depressing.

               27

28 When he takes a holiday, Martin prefers to

    A   relax by the sea.

    B   stay in comfortable surroundings.

    C   travel for a particular reason.

               28

29 Martin thought that the holiday-makers he saw in the Dominican Republic were

    A   risking their health.

    B   wasting opportunities.

    C   lacking entertainment.

               29

30 What is Martin's opinion of tourism?

    A   It should be discouraged.

    B   It can be a good thing.

    C   It is well managed.

               30

PAPER 5 SPEAKING (14 minutes)

You take the Speaking test with another candidate, referred to here as your partner. There are two examiners. One will speak to you and your partner and the other will be listening. Both examiners will award marks.

Part 1 (3 minutes)

The examiner asks you and your partner questions about yourselves. You may be asked about things like 'your home town', 'your interests', 'your career plans', etc.

Part 2 (4 minutes)

The examiner gives you two photographs and asks you to talk about them for one minute. The examiner then asks your partner a question about your photographs and your partner responds briefly.

Then the examiner gives your partner two different photographs. Your partner talks about these photographs for one minute. This time the examiner asks you a question about your partner's photographs and you respond briefly.

Part 3 (approximately 3 minutes)

The examiner asks you and your partner to talk together. You may be asked to solve a problem or try to come to a decision about something. For example, you might be asked to decide the best way to use some rooms in a language school. The examiner gives you a picture to help you but does not join in the conversation.

Part 4 (approximately 4 minutes)

The examiner joins in the conversation. You all talk together in a more general way about what has been said in Part 3. The examiner asks you questions but you and your partner are also expected to develop the conversation.

Test 4

PAPER 1 READING (1 hour 15 minutes)

Part 1

You are going to read a magazine article about a man who teaches children how to improve their memory. Choose the most suitable heading from the list **A–I** for each part (**1–7**) of the article. There is one extra heading which you do not need to use. There is an example at the beginning (**0**).

Mark your answers **on the separate answer sheet**.

A	An obvious need
B	Gaining attention
C	The odder the better
D	Making sense of information
E	Trade secrets
F	Academic approval
G	A change of focus
H	Selected memories
I	An ancient skill

Memory test

Jerome Burne talks to a magician who teaches children ways to remember facts.

0	I

The Greek philosophers knew about it and it could still dramatically improve children's school results today, except that no one teaches it. 'It' is a very old technique for making your memory better. Try memorising this series of random numbers: 3,6,5,5,2,1,2,4. About as meaningful as dates in history or equations in maths, aren't they? Chances are you won't remember them in five minutes, let alone in five hours. However, had you been at a lecture given at a school in the south of England last month, you would now be able to fix them in your head for five days, five weeks, in fact for ever.

1	

'I am going to give you five techniques that will enable you to remember anything you need to know at school,' promised lecturer Ian Robinson to a fascinated audience of a hundred schoolchildren. He slapped his hand down on the table. In his other life, Robinson is an entertainer, and he was using all the tricks he had picked up in his career. 'When I've finished in two hours' time, your work will be far more effective and productive. Anyone not interested, leave now.' The entire room sat still, glued to their seats.

2	

When he entertains, Robinson calls himself the Mind Magician. He specialises in doing magic tricks that look totally impossible, and then he reveals that they involve nothing more mysterious than good old-fashioned trickery. 'I have always been interested in tricks involving memory – being able to reel off the order of cards in a pack, that sort of thing,' he explains.

3	

Robinson was already lecturing to schools on his magic techniques when it struck him that students might find memory techniques even more valuable. 'It wasn't a difficult area to move into, as the stuff's all there in books.' So he summarised everything to make a two-hour lecture about five techniques.

4	

What Robinson's schoolchildren get are methods that will be familiar to anyone who has dipped into any one of a dozen books on memory. The difference is that Robinson's approach is firmly aimed at schoolchildren. The basic idea is to take material that is random and meaningless – musical scales, the bones of the arm – and give them a structure. That series of numbers at the beginning of the article fits in here. Once you think of it as the number of days in the year – 365 – and the number of weeks – 52 – and so on, it suddenly becomes permanently memorable.

5	

'You want to learn a list of a hundred things? A thousand? No problem,' says Robinson. The scandal is that every child is not taught the techniques from the beginning of their school life. The schoolchildren who were watching him thought it was brilliant. 'I wish I'd been told this earlier,' commented Mark, after Robinson had shown them how to construct 'mental journeys'.

6	

Essentially, you visualise a walk down a street, or a trip round a room, and pick the points where you will put the things you want to remember – the lamppost, the fruit bowl. Then in each location you put a visual representation of your list – phrasal verbs, historical dates, whatever – making them as strange as possible. It is that simple, and it works.

7	

The reaction of schools has been uniformly enthusiastic. 'The pupils benefited enormously from Ian's presentation,' says Dr Johnston, head of the school where Robinson was speaking. 'Ideally we should run a regular class in memory techniques so pupils can pick it up gradually.'

Part 2

You are going to read an article about the actress Harriet Walter. For questions **8–15**, choose the answer (**A, B, C** or **D**) which you think fits best according to the text.

Mark your answers **on the separate answer sheet**.

Acting minus the drama

Harriet Walter has written a fascinating book about her profession.
Benedicte Page reports.

It is not often that an experienced actor with a high public profile will sit down to answer in depth the ordinary theatregoer's questions: how do you put together a character which isn't your own?; what is it like to perform the same play night after night?; or simply, why do you do it? Harriet Walter was prompted to write *Other People's Shoes: Thoughts on Acting* by a sense that many people's interest in theatre extended beyond the scope of entertainment chit-chat. 'I was asked very intelligent, probing questions by people who weren't in the profession, from taxi drivers to dinner-party hosts to people in shopping queues. It made me realise that people have an interest in what we do which goes beyond show-business gossip,' she says.

Other People's Shoes avoids insider gossip and, mostly, autobiography: 'If events in my life had had a huge direct influence, I would have put them in, but they didn't,' Harriet says, though she does explain how her parents' divorce was a factor in her career. But the focus of the book is to share – remarkably openly – the inside experience of the stage and the rehearsal room, aiming to replace the false sense of mystery with a more realistic understanding and respect for the profession.

'There's a certain double edge to the publicity an actor can get in the newspapers: it gives you attention but, by giving it to you, simultaneously criticises you,' Harriet says. 'People ask you to talk about yourself and then say, "Oh, actors are so self-centred." And the "sound-bite" variety of journalism, which touches on many things but never allows you to go into them in depth, leaves you with a sort of shorthand which reinforces prejudices and myths.'

Harriet's career began in the 1970s and has included theatre performances with the Royal Shakespeare Company and television and film roles. She writes wittily about the embarrassments of the rehearsal room, as actors try out their half-formed ideas. And she is at pains to demystify the theatre: the question 'How do you do the same play every night?' is answered by a simple comparison with the familiar car journey you take every day, which presents a slightly different challenge each time. 'I was trying to get everyone to understand it isn't this extraordinary mystery and you're not visited by some spiritual inspiration every night.'

Harriet's own acting style is to build up a character piece by piece. She says that this process is not widely understood: 'There's no intelligent vocabulary out there for discussing the craft of building characters. Reviews of an actor's performance which appear in the newspapers are generally based on whether the reviewer likes the actors or not. It's not about whether they are being skilful or not, or how intelligent their choices are.'

There remains something mysterious about slipping into 'other people's shoes': 'It's something like falling in love,' Harriet says. 'When you're in love with someone, you go in and out of separateness and togetherness. It's similar with acting and you can slip in and out of a character. Once a character has been built, it remains with you, at the end of a phone line, as it were, waiting for your call.'

Harriet includes her early work in *Other People's Shoes* – 'I wanted to separate myself from those who say, "What an idiot I was, what a load of nonsense we all talked in those days!"; it wasn't all rubbish, and it has affected how I approach my work and my audiences.' And she retains from those days her belief in the vital role of the theatre.

line 54

8   Harriet Walter decided to write her book because she

    A   was tired of answering people's questions about acting.

    B   knew people liked to read about showbusiness gossip.

    C   wanted to entertain people through her writing.

    D   wanted to satisfy people's curiosity about acting in the theatre.

9   In paragraph two, we learn that Harriet's book aims to

    A   correct some of the impressions people have of the theatre.

    B   relate important details about her own life story.

    C   analyse the difficulties of a career in the theatre.

    D   tell the truth about some of the actors she has worked with.

10   What problem do actors have with newspaper publicity?

    A   It never focuses on the actors who deserve it.

    B   It often does more harm than good.

    C   It never reports what actors have actually said.

    D   It often makes mistakes when reporting facts.

11   Harriet uses the example of the car journey to show that

    A   acting can be boring as well as rewarding.

    B   actors do not find it easy to try new ideas.

    C   actors do not deserve the praise they receive.

    D   acting shares characteristics with other repetitive activities.

12   What does 'it' refer to in line 54?

    A   facing a different challenge

    B   taking a familiar car journey

    C   acting in the same play every night

    D   working with fellow actors

13   Harriet criticises theatre reviewers because they

    A   do not give enough recognition to the art of character acting.

    B   do not realise that some parts are more difficult to act than others.

    C   choose the wrong kinds of plays to review.

    D   suggest that certain actors have an easy job.

14   Harriet says that after actors have played a particular character, they

    A   may be asked to play other similar characters.

    B   may become a bit like the character.

    C   will never want to play the part again.

    D   will never forget how to play the part.

15   What does Harriet say about her early work?

    A   It has been a valuable influence on the work she has done since.

    B   It was completely different from the kind of work she does now.

    C   She finds it embarrassing to recall that period of her life.

    D   She is annoyed when people criticise the work she did then.

Part 3

You are going to read a newspaper article about a man who is running round the world. Eight paragraphs have been removed from the article. Choose from the paragraphs **A–I** the one which fits each gap (**16–22**). There is one extra paragraph which you do not need to use. There is an example at the beginning (**0**).

Mark your answers **on the separate answer sheet**.

The Runningman

Bryan Green, a 32-year-old from London, calls himself the 'Runningman'. He runs and keeps on running through towns, cities, up mountains and across rivers. Green has set his sights on running round the world.

| **0** | **I** |

He then flew to the north of Japan and ran to Osaka in the south. In Australia he ran from Perth to Sydney, and then he began in the Americas, bringing his current total to 23 countries, 45,000 kilometres and 30 pairs of trainers.

| **16** | |

When I met Green in Rio, he had just run 70 kilometres, his daily average. He was holding in one hand a two-litre bottle of fizzy juice and in the other a piece of paper that he needed someone to sign, to confirm the time at which he had arrived.

| **17** | |

He travels light, carrying with him less than many people take to work. In his backpack he has a palmtop computer, a digital video camera, a Nikon 35mm camera, a map, a toothbrush and one change of clothes.

| **18** | |

'The original idea was just to see the world,' he told me. 'But, as I soon realised, I could make myself a future. I have learnt how to make money out of what I do.' He started off with £20 in his pocket and estimates that he has earned about £60,000 so far.

| **19** | |

And there is something of the explorer about him. 'Of course, I've found some places easier than others,' he says.

| **20** | |

At one point on that stage of the journey, Green got lost and was unable to find enough to eat. But generally he has been lucky with his health: he has not been injured and has never fallen ill.

| **21** | |

He speaks no language apart from English and, with no space for a dictionary, has a plastic-covered sheet of A4 paper with a dozen useful phrases in various languages. Over dinner he is keen to talk about the Amazon jungle.

| **22** | |

However, perhaps the point of a run like Green's is not to indulge in proper preparation. Its beauty is in the improvisation. 'I don't really analyse the run any more, I just do it,' he says.

A I did it for him. Even though he already holds the world long-distance running record, he still needs to continue proving he is keeping up a reasonable running speed.

B He has not yet sorted out a route and appears surprised when I tell him that there are no proper roads across it, as local people prefer to use the rivers instead.

C He's done this by selling his story to journalists. He is very aware that he is a marketable product.

D He has learned that you must take only what you will use. He has no medical supplies and no proper waterproofs.

E Apart from the day in south Australia where it was 45 °C in the shade and he collapsed, Australia is, he says, perfect running country. This compares to his experiences in temperatures of –30 °C in parts of Asia.

F Next week he heads off north, towards the Amazon, hoping to run to New York. After that, he just has to take care of Africa and Antarctica.

G So he is a touchingly solitary figure. He is too mobile to be able to make many friends, although he did meet someone in Australia who cycled next to him for 600 kilometres.

H Fortunately, the cold and the rain don't seem to bother him. It is partly his strength of character that made him refuse to take health insurance.

I The Runningman recently arrived in Rio de Janeiro in Brazil via a roundabout route: he left London four years ago and ran through Europe to China.

Part 4

You are going to read an article about people who changed their jobs. For questions **23–35**, choose from the people (**A–D**). The people may be chosen more than once. There is an example at the beginning (**0**).

Mark your answers **on the separate answer sheet**.

Which person mentions

enjoying their pastime more than the job they used to do?	**0**	**B**
enjoying being in charge of their own life?	**23**	
being surprised by suddenly losing their previous job?	**24**	
not having other people depending on them financially?	**25**	
missing working with other people?	**26**	
undergoing training in order to take up their new job?	**27**	
a contact being useful in promoting their new business?	**28**	
not being interested in possible promotion in their old job?	**29**	
disliking the amount of time they used to have to work?	**30**	
surprising someone else by the decision they made?	**31**	
a prediction that hasn't come true?	**32**	
consulting other people about their businesses?	**33**	
the similarities between their new job and their old one?	**34**	
working to a strict timetable?	**35**	

A NEW LIFE

A   The Farmer

Matt Froggatt used to be an insurance agent in the City of London but now runs a sheep farm.

'After 14 years in business, I found that the City had gone from a place which was exciting to work in to a grind – no one was having fun any more. But I hadn't planned to leave for another five or ten years when I was made redundant. It came out of the blue, but it made me take a careful look at my life. I didn't get a particularly good pay-off but it was enough to set up the farm with. My break came when I got to know the head chef of a local hotel with one of the top 20 hotel restaurants in the country. Through supplying them, my reputation spread and now I also supply meat through mail order. I'm glad I'm no longer stuck in the office but it's astonishing how little things have changed for me: the same 80- to 90-hour week and still selling a product.'

B   The Painter

Ron Ablewhite was a manager in advertising but now makes a living as an artist.

'My painting began as a hobby but I realised I was getting far more excitement out of it than out of working. The decision to take redundancy and to become an artist seemed logical. The career counsellor I talked to was very helpful. I think I was the first person who had ever told him, "I don't want to go back to where I've been." He was astonished because the majority of people in their mid-forties need to get back to work immediately – they need the money. But we had married young and our children didn't need our support. It was a leap into the unknown. We went to the north of England, where we didn't know a soul. It meant leaving all our friends, but we've been lucky in that our friendships have survived the distance – plenty of them come up and visit us now.'

C   The Hatmaker

After working for five years as a company lawyer, Katherine Goodison set up her own business in her London flat, making hats for private clients.

'My job as a lawyer was fun. It was stimulating and I earned a lot of money, but the hours were terrible. I realised I didn't want to become a senior partner in the company, working more and more hours, so I left. A lot of people said I'd get bored, but that has never happened. The secret is to have deadlines. Since it's a fashion-related business, you have the collections, next year's shapes, the season – there's always too much to do, so you have to run a very regimented diary. I feel happier now, and definitely less stressed. There are things I really long for, though, like the social interaction with colleagues. What I love about this job is that I'm totally responsible for the product. If I do a rubbish job, then I'm the one who takes the blame. Of course, you care when you're working for a company, but when your name is all over the promotional material, you care that little bit more.'

D   The Masseur

Paul Drinkwater worked in finance for 16 years before becoming a masseur at the Life Centre in London.

'I had been in financial markets from the age of 22, setting up deals. I liked the adrenaline but I never found the work rewarding. I was nearly made redundant in 1989, but I escaped by resigning and travelling for a year. I spent that year trying to work out what I wanted to do. I was interested in health, so I visited some of the world's best gymnasiums and talked to the owners about how they started up. I knew that to change career I had to get qualifications so I did various courses in massage. Then I was offered part-time work at the Life Centre. I have no regrets. I never used to feel in control, but now I have peace of mind and control of my destiny. That's best of all.'

PAPER 2   WRITING (1 hour 30 minutes)

Part 1

You **must** answer this question.

---

1   Your English friend, Kim, has written to you asking you if you'd like to go to a concert by your favourite band, Red Stone.

Read Kim's letter, on which you have made some notes. Then write a letter to Kim accepting the invitation and giving all the necessary information. You must use all your notes.

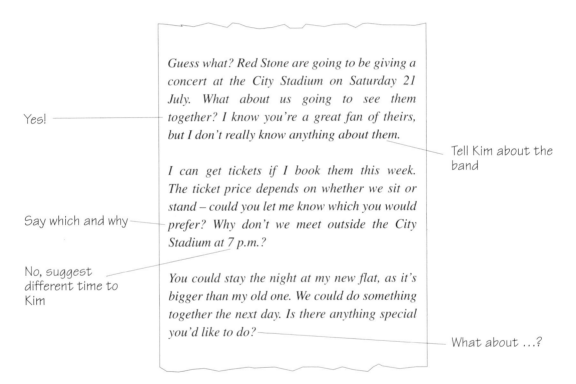

Yes!

Guess what? Red Stone are going to be giving a concert at the City Stadium on Saturday 21 July. What about us going to see them together? I know you're a great fan of theirs, but I don't really know anything about them.

Tell Kim about the band

Say which and why

I can get tickets if I book them this week. The ticket price depends on whether we sit or stand – could you let me know which you would prefer? Why don't we meet outside the City Stadium at 7 p.m.?

No, suggest different time to Kim

You could stay the night at my new flat, as it's bigger than my old one. We could do something together the next day. Is there anything special you'd like to do?

What about …?

Write a **letter** of between **120** and **180** words in an appropriate style.
Do not write any postal addresses.

Part 2

Write an answer to **one** of the questions **2–5** in this part. Write your answer in **120–180** words in an appropriate style.

---

2   Your teacher has asked you for a report on transport in your local area. Mention the main means of transport used, and suggest how transport facilities could be improved.

Write your **report**.

3   You see this notice on your school noticeboard.

SPECIAL PEOPLE

- Who is the most important person in your life?

- Why is this person special to you?

Write us an article for the school magazine answering these questions.

Write your **article**.

4   Your teacher has asked you to write a story for the school's English language magazine. The story must **begin** with the following words:

My day started badly, but it got better and better.

Write your **story**.

5   Answer **one** of the following two questions based on your reading of **one** of these set books. Write the letter **(a)** or **(b)** as well as the number **5** in the question box, and the **title** of the book next to the box. Your answer **must** be about one of the books below.

Best Detective Stories of Agatha Christie – Longman Fiction
Round the World in Eighty Days – Jules Verne
A Tale of Two Cities – Charles Dickens
Animal Farm – George Orwell
More Tales from Shakespeare – Charles and Mary Lamb

Either   **(a)**   What was the most unexpected event in the book or short story you have read? Write a **composition** for your teacher describing what happened and explaining why you were surprised.

Or   **(b)**   An international magazine is publishing articles about its readers' favourite books. Write an **article** explaining why the book or collection of short stories you have read is one of your favourite books.

PAPER 3 USE OF ENGLISH (1 hour 15 minutes)

Part 1

For questions **1–15**, read the text below and decide which answer (**A**, **B**, **C** or **D**) best fits each space. There is an example at the beginning (**0**).

Mark your answers **on the separate answer sheet.**

Example:

0   A priceless   **B** rewarding   **C** precious   **D** prized

0	A	B	C	D
	⸺	▬	⸺	⸺

MOUNTAIN CLIMBING

One of the most difficult but **(0)** ..... of pastimes is the sport of mountain climbing. Mountain climbing can be divided into two categories, rock climbing and ice climbing, and the modern climber must **(1)** ..... many different skills.

Rock climbing **(2)** ..... a combination of gymnastic ability, imagination and observation, but perhaps the most necessary skill is being able to **(3)** ..... out how much weight a particular rock will **(4)** ..... . Mountaineers climb in groups of three or four, each climber at a distance of approximately six metres from the next. Usually one person climbs while the other climbers **(5)** ..... hold of the rope. The most experienced climber goes first and **(6)** ..... the other climbers which **(7)** ..... to go. When the leader has reached a good position, he or she makes the rope secure so that it is **(8)** ..... for the others to follow.

Since much mountain climbing **(9)** ..... place in bad weather, snow skills **(10)** ..... a very important part. Ice axes are used for **(11)** ..... steps into the snow, and for testing the ground. Climbers always tie themselves **(12)** ..... , so that, if the leader does fall, he or she can be held by the others and **(13)** ..... back to safety. The number of dangers **(14)** ..... by climbers is almost endless. Yet perhaps the most difficult part of the sport is the physical effort needed when the air has little oxygen. The **(15)** ..... of oxygen can leave mountaineers continually out of breath.

1 **A** own   **B** hold   **C** control   **D** possess

2 **A** requires   **B** insists   **C** calls   **D** orders

3 **A** work   **B** try   **C** stand   **D** set

4 **A** supply   **B** provide   **C** support   **D** offer

5 **A** keep   **B** stay   **C** continue   **D** maintain

6 **A** indicates   **B** signals   **C** points   **D** shows

7 **A** passage   **B** way   **C** walk   **D** course

8 **A** safe   **B** sure   **C** dependable   **D** reliable

9 **A** gets   **B** takes   **C** occupies   **D** fills

10 **A** act   **B** do   **C** play   **D** make

11 **A** cutting   **B** tearing   **C** breaking   **D** splitting

12 **A** collectively **B** jointly   **C** together   **D** co-operatively

13 **A** given   **B** pulled   **C** put   **D** sent

14 **A** marked   **B** touched   **C** felt   **D** faced

15 **A** need   **B** gap   **C** lack   **D** demand

Part 2

For questions **16–30**, read the text below and think of the word which best fits each space. Use only **one** word in each space. There is an example at the beginning (**0**).

Write your answers **on the separate answer sheet**.

Example: | **0** | *of* |

A NEW CRUISE SHIP

One (**0**) ....*of*.... the biggest passenger ships in history, the *Island Princess*, carries people on cruises around the Caribbean. More than double (**16**) .... weight of the *Titanic* (the large passenger ship which sank in 1912), it was (**17**) .... large to be built in (**18**) .... piece. Instead, forty-eight sections (**19**) .... total were made in different places. The ship was then put together (**20**) .... these sections at a shipbuilding yard in Italy.

The huge weight of the *Island Princess* is partly due to her enormous height, (**21**) .... is an incredible forty-one metres. When compared with the *Titanic*, she is also a much broader ship. As (**22**) .... as length is concerned, there's (**23**) .... a great difference, each ship (**24**) .... over two hundred and fifty metres long.

The *Island Princess* can carry (**25**) .... to 2,600 passengers and has 1,321 cabins, including twenty-five specially designed (**26**) .... use by disabled passengers. There is entertainment on board to suit (**27**) .... age and interest, from dancing to good drama. The *Island Princess* seems very likely to be a popular holiday choice for many years to (**28**) .... , even though most people will (**29**) .... to save up in order to be (**30**) .... to afford the trip.

Part 3

For questions **31–40**, complete the second sentence so that it has a similar meaning to the first sentence, using the word given. **Do not change the word given**. You must use between **two** and **five** words, including the word given.

Here is an example (**0**).

Example:

0 You must do exactly what the manager tells you.

carry

You must .... instructions exactly.

The space can be filled by the words 'carry out the manager's' so you write:

0	*carry out the manager's*

Write **only** the missing words on **the separate answer sheet**.

---

31 As a result of the strong wind last night, several tiles came off the roof.

because

Several tiles came off the roof .... so strong last night.

32 In my opinion, Ali is clearly going to be very successful.

doubt

I .... that Ali is going to be very successful.

33 Simona last wrote to me seven months ago.

heard

I .... Simona for seven months.

34 I don't recommend hiring skis at this shop.

advisable

It's .... skis at this shop.

35 Mike's father started the company that Mike now runs.

   set

   The company that Mike now runs .... his father.

36 The number of car-owners has risen over the past five years.

   rise

   Over the past five years, there .... in the number of car-owners.

37 'Don't worry Mum, I can look after myself now I'm sixteen,' said Peter.

   care

   Peter assured his mother that he could .... now he was sixteen.

38 Naomi said that she would never talk to anyone else about the matter.

   discuss

   Naomi promised never .... anyone else.

39 'This is the best hotel I've ever stayed in,' my colleague said.

   never

   'I've .... hotel than this,' my colleague said.

40 There were very few people at the concert last night.

   came

   Hardly .... the concert last night.

Part 4

For questions **41–55**, read the text below and look carefully at each line. Some of the lines are correct, and some have a word which should not be there.

If a line is correct, put a tick (✓) by the number **on the separate answer sheet**. If a line has a word which should **not** be there, write the word **on the separate answer sheet**. There are two examples at the beginning (**0** and **00**).

0	✓

Examples:

00	*did*

THE TRAIN JOURNEY

0	You know I was going down to London to stay with my friend
00	Alice during the holidays. Well, the train journey did turned out
41	to be a bit of a disaster! I went to a party the night before I had left,
42	and I woke up quite late enough, so I had to catch the train that
43	left round about midday. At first, I enjoyed the journey as there was
44	another student sitting opposite of me and we started talking.
45	Anyway, when she got out of the train at Oxford, I decided to read
46	my book but, because I hadn't had much sleep on the night before,
47	I soon fell asleep. I must have to slept for over an hour, because
48	I was woke up when all the doors started banging and I realised
49	that everyone was getting out because we were once in London.
50	I jumped up and managed to get myself and my luggage out in
51	a couple of seconds, and breathed a huge sigh of relief. It
52	was only when I had arrived at Alice's house that I have realised I
53	had dropped my address book down when I was getting out of
54	the train. It's a good thing I can properly remember your address,
55	otherwise I wouldn't have been able to write it to you, would I?

Part 5

For questions **56–65**, read the text below. Use the word given in capitals at the end of each line to form a word that fits in the space in the **same** line. There is an example at the beginning (**0**).

Write your answers **on the separate answer sheet**.

Example:

0	*excitement*

PUTTING ON A STAGE SHOW

The opening night of a stage show means (**0**) ...*excitement*... and glamour. **EXCITE**

Often it also means (**56**) .... problems suddenly arising. And that is even **EXPECT**

more true if you are planning to take 50 total (**57**) .... and produce the **STRANGE**

(**58**) .... *South Pacific* in two days. But that's what mother-and-daughter **MUSIC**

team Linda and Nicki Metz are (**59**) .... offering as a weekend course. **CURRENT**

The plan seems (**60**) .... , although the two leading parts in the show will be **AMBITION**

taken by (**61**) .... actors. Technical staff will be on hand to give expert **PROFESSION**

advice to (**62**) .... Linda says: 'It will be a great weekend for people to do **PERFORM**

something (**63**) .... and achieve something at the same time. People have **ENJOY**

a (**64**) .... to work better if they have a deadline. A lot of people also **TEND**

discover talents that they were (**65**) .... of.' **AWARE**

PAPER 4   LISTENING (approximately 40 minutes)

Part 1

You will hear people talking in eight different situations. For questions **1–8**, choose the best answer (**A**, **B** or **C**).

---

1   On a train, you overhear a woman phoning her office.
    Why has she phoned?

   A   to check the time of an appointment

   B   to apologise for being late

   C   to find out where her diary is

   1

2   You switch on the radio in the middle of a programme.
    What kind of programme is it?

   A   a nature programme

   B   a cookery programme

   C   a news programme

   2

3   You overhear a conversation between a watchmaker and a customer.
    What does the watchmaker say about the watch?

   A   It is impossible to repair it.

   B   It is not worth repairing.

   C   He does not have the parts to repair it.

   3

4   You overhear a woman talking about her new neighbours.
    How does she feel?

   A   offended

   B   shocked

   C   suspicious

   4

5   You hear a man talking about deep-sea diving.
    Why does he like the sport?

    A   It suits his sociable nature.

    B   It contrasts with his normal lifestyle. | 5 |

    C   It fulfils his need for a challenge in life.

6   You turn on the radio and hear a scientist being interviewed about violins.
    What is the scientist doing?

    A   explaining how a violin works

    B   explaining how a violin is made | 6 |

    C   explaining how a violin should be played

7   You hear part of a radio programme about CD ROMs.
    What is the speaker's opinion of the CD ROMs about Australia which she tried?

    A   Most of them are disappointing.

    B   You are better off with an ordinary guidebook. | 7 |

    C   There is little difference between them.

8   You turn on the radio and hear a woman giving advice to business people.
    What advice does she give about dealing with customers?

    A   Don't let them force you to agree to something.

    B   Don't be too sympathetic towards them. | 8 |

    C   Don't allow them to stay on the phone too long.

Part 2

You will hear part of a radio programme in which a woman called Sylvia Short is interviewed about her job. For questions **9–18**, complete the sentences.

Sylvia studied | *and* | **9** | at university.

After university, Sylvia worked as a | **10** | in Italy.

The company which employs Sylvia is called | **11**

Sylvia worked for the company for

| **12** | before becoming the manager's assistant.

Part of Sylvia's job is to organise the

| **13** | in newspapers and magazines.

Sylvia often has to deal with strange questions from | **14**

Sylvia's boss has a radio show on Fridays on the subject of

| **15**

Sylvia has written about her

| **16** | for a new book on Britain.

Sylvia says that in the future she would like to be a

| **17** | on television.

Last year, Sylvia enjoyed attending a | **18** | in Australia.

Part 3

You will hear five different people speaking on the subject of motorbikes. For questions **19–23**, choose the phrase (**A–F**) which best summarises what each speaker is talking about. Use the letters only once. There is one extra letter which you do not need to use.

A   the perfect passenger

                                                               Speaker 1   **19**

B   a feeling of power

                                                               Speaker 2   **20**

C   a lengthy career

                                                               Speaker 3   **21**

D   the best way to learn

                                                               Speaker 4   **22**

E   a family business

                                                               Speaker 5   **23**

F   a break with routine

Part 4

You will hear part of a radio interview with Steve Thomas, a young chef who has his own cookery series on television. For questions **24–30**, choose the best answer (**A, B** or **C**).

24 On his TV programme, Steve likes to show audiences

    A   the process of cooking.

    B   amusing incidents.

    C   attractively presented dishes.

	24

25 Steve was given his own TV series because

    A   he cooked for a TV company.

    B   he appeared on a TV programme.

    C   he had been recommended to a TV producer.

	25

26 What made him take up cooking as a child?

    A   His parents expected him to help in their restaurant.

    B   He felt it was the best way of getting some money.

    C   His father wanted to teach him to cook.

	26

27 How did Steve feel once he got to college?

    A   He still found academic work difficult.

    B   He regretted not studying harder at school.

    C   He was confident about his practical work.

	27

28 What does Steve say about the cooks who work for him?

    A   He is sometimes unfair to them.

    B   He demands a lot from them.

    C   He trains them all himself.

	28

29 Steve admires Ron Bell because

    A   he prepares traditional dishes.

    B   he writes excellent articles about food.

    C   he makes a point of using local produce.

	29

30 How will Steve's book be different from other books about cooking?

    A   the varieties of food it deals with

    B   the way that it is illustrated

    C   the sort of person it is aimed at

	30

PAPER 5   SPEAKING (14 minutes)

You take the Speaking test with another candidate, referred to here as your partner. There are two examiners. One will speak to you and your partner and the other will be listening. Both examiners will award marks.

Part 1 (3 minutes)

The examiner asks you and your partner questions about yourselves. You may be asked about things like 'your home town', 'your interests', 'your career plans', etc.

Part 2 (4 minutes)

The examiner gives you two photographs and asks you to talk about them for one minute. The examiner then asks your partner a question about your photographs and your partner responds briefly.

Then the examiner gives your partner two different photographs. Your partner talks about these photographs for one minute. This time the examiner asks you a question about your partner's photographs and you respond briefly.

Part 3 (approximately 3 minutes)

The examiner asks you and your partner to talk together. You may be asked to solve a problem or try to come to a decision about something. For example, you might be asked to decide the best way to use some rooms in a language school. The examiner gives you a picture to help you but does not join in the conversation.

Part 4 (approximately 4 minutes)

The examiner joins in the conversation. You all talk together in a more general way about what has been said in Part 3. The examiner asks you questions but you and your partner are also expected to develop the conversation.

 **UNIVERSITY** *of* **CAMBRIDGE**
ESOL Examinations

S A M P L E

Candidate Name
If not already printed, write name
in CAPITALS and complete the
Candidate No. grid (in pencil).

Candidate Signature

Examination Title

Centre

Supervisor:
If the candidate is ABSENT or has WITHDRAWN shade here ▭

Centre No.

Candidate No.

Examination Details

0	0	0	0
1	1	1	1
2	2	2	2
3	3	3	3
4	4	4	4
5	5	5	5
6	6	6	6
7	7	7	7
8	8	8	8
9	9	9	9

Candidate Answer Sheet: FCE Paper 1 Reading

Use a pencil

Mark ONE letter for each question.

For example, if you think B is the right answer to the question, mark your answer sheet like this:

0 A B C D E F G H I

Rub out any answer you wish to change with an eraser.

1	A B C D E F G H I
2	A B C D E F G H I
3	A B C D E F G H I
4	A B C D E F G H I
5	A B C D E F G H I

6	A B C D E F G H I
7	A B C D E F G H I
8	A B C D E F G H I
9	A B C D E F G H I
10	A B C D E F G H I
11	A B C D E F G H I
12	A B C D E F G H I
13	A B C D E F G H I
14	A B C D E F G H I
15	A B C D E F G H I
16	A B C D E F G H I
17	A B C D E F G H I
18	A B C D E F G H I
19	A B C D E F G H I
20	A B C D E F G H I

21	A B C D E F G H I
22	A B C D E F G H I
23	A B C D E F G H I
24	A B C D E F G H I
25	A B C D E F G H I
26	A B C D E F G H I
27	A B C D E F G H I
28	A B C D E F G H I
29	A B C D E F G H I
30	A B C D E F G H I
31	A B C D E F G H I
32	A B C D E F G H I
33	A B C D E F G H I
34	A B C D E F G H I
35	A B C D E F G H I

UNIVERSITY *of* **CAMBRIDGE**
ESOL Examinations

S A M P L E

Candidate Name
If not already printed, write name
in CAPITALS and complete the
Candidate No. grid (in pencil)

Centre No.

Candidate Signature

Candidate No.

Examination Title

Examination Details

Centre

Supervisor:

If the candidate is ABSENT or has WITHDRAWN shade here

0	0	0	0
1	1	1	1
2	2	2	2
3	3	3	3
4	4	4	4
5	5	5	5
6	6	6	6
7	7	7	7
8	8	8	8
9	9	9	9

Candidate Answer Sheet: FCE Paper 3 Use of English

Use a **PENCIL** (B or HB). Rub out any answer you wish to change with an eraser.

For **Part 1**: Mark ONE letter for each question.
For example, if you think **C** is the right answer to the question, mark your answer sheet like this:

For **Parts 2, 3, 4** and **5**: Write your answers in the spaces next to the numbers like this:

| 0 | A | B | C | D |

| 0 | example |

Part 1

1	A B C D
2	A B C D
3	A B C D
4	A B C D
5	A B C D
6	A B C D
7	A B C D
8	A B C D
9	A B C D
10	A B C D
11	A B C D
12	A B C D
13	A B C D
14	A B C D
15	A B C D

Part 2

		Do not write here
16		1 16 0
17		1 17 0
18		1 18 0
19		1 19 0
20		1 20 0
21		1 21 0
22		1 22 0
23		1 23 0
24		1 24 0
25		1 25 0
26		1 26 0
27		1 27 0
28		1 28 0
29		1 29 0
30		1 30 0

Turn over for Parts 3 - 5
→

Part 3

		Do not write here
31		31 0 1 2
32		32 0 1 2
33		33 0 1 2
34		34 0 1 2
35		35 0 1 2
36		36 0 1 2
37		37 0 1 2
38		38 0 1 2
39		39 0 1 2
40		40 0 1 2

Part 4

		Do not write here
41		1 41 0
42		1 42 0
43		1 43 0
44		1 44 0
45		1 45 0
46		1 46 0
47		1 47 0
48		1 48 0
49		1 49 0
50		1 50 0
51		1 51 0
52		1 52 0
53		1 53 0
54		1 54 0
55		1 55 0

Part 5

		Do not write here
56		1 56 0
57		1 57 0
58		1 58 0
59		1 59 0
60		1 60 0
61		1 61 0
62		1 62 0
63		1 63 0
64		1 64 0
65		1 65 0

Sample answer sheet: Paper 4

 **UNIVERSITY** *of* **CAMBRIDGE**
ESOL Examinations

S A M P L E

■   ■

Candidate Name
If not already printed, write name
in CAPITALS and complete the
Candidate No. grid (in pencil).

Candidate Signature

Examination Title

Centre

Supervisor:

If the candidate is ABSENT or has WITHDRAWN shade here ▭

Centre No.

Candidate No.

**Examination
Details**

0	0	0	0
1	1	1	1
2	2	2	2
3	3	3	3
4	4	4	4
5	5	5	5
6	6	6	6
7	7	7	7
8	8	8	8
9	9	9	9

Candidate Answer Sheet: FCE Paper 4 Listening

Mark test version (in PENCIL)

A	B	C	D	E
J	K			
Special arrangements	S	H		

Instructions

Use a PENCIL.
Rub out any answer you
wish to change using an
eraser.

For **Parts 1** and **3**:
Mark ONE letter for each
question.

For example, if you think
B is the right answer to
the question, mark your
answer sheet like this:

| 0 | A | B | C |

For **Part 2**:
Write your answer clearly
in the space like this:

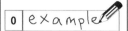
| 0 | example |

For **Part 4**:
Write ONE letter only.

Part 1

1	A	B	C
2	A	B	C
3	A	B	C
4	A	B	C
5	A	B	C
6	A	B	C
7	A	B	C
8	A	B	C

Part 2

9		1 9 0
10		1 10 0
11		1 11 0
12		1 12 0
13		1 13 0
14		1 14 0
15		1 15 0
16		1 16 0
17		1 17 0
18		1 18 0

Do not
write here

Part 3

19	A	B	C	D	E	F
20	A	B	C	D	E	F
21	A	B	C	D	E	F
22	A	B	C	D	E	F
23	A	B	C	D	E	F

Part 4

24		1 24 0
25		1 25 0
26		1 26 0
27		1 27 0
28		1 28 0
29		1 29 0
30		1 30 0

Do not
write here

© UCLES 2004 Photocopiable

100